In Need of Special Understanding

Camphill conferences on living with handicapped adults

Karl König M.D. (Vienna)

IN NEED OF
SPECIAL UNDERSTANDING

Camphill conferences on living with handicapped adults

The Image of Man as it pertains to our villagers
9th–12th January 1962

The Threefold Constitution of Man
29th January–1st February 1963

Learning and Working — the Karma of Vocation
18th–20th January 1964

KARL KÖNIG

Edited by Hubert Zipperlen

Camphill Press

1st Edition 1986

Published by Camphill Press
on behalf of
The Association of Camphill Communities

© 1986 Trustees of the Karl König Archive

British Library Cataloguing in Publication Data

König, Karl
   In need of special understanding : Camphill conferences
on living with handicapped adults.
1. Mentally handicapped — Great Britain — Home care
I. Title   II. Zipperlen, Hubert
362.3'0941   HV3008.G7

ISBN 0–904145–26–3
ISBN 0–904145–27–1 Pbk

MADE AND PRINTED IN GREAT BRITAIN
BY CAMPHILL PRESS, BOTTON VILLAGE
DANBY, WHITBY, N. YORKS. YO21 2NJ

Foreword

The following lectures and discussions were held in three successive years between 1962 and 1964 for co-workers in the few recently founded Camphill villages in Britain for and with handicapped adults. These villages all tried to establish workshops, farms, households and a small measure of adult education. The living conditions were poor—subsidies from the State only came slowly later—and these lectures therefore gave tremendous encouragement, albeit from an unexpected direction, for our will to find a new life together with handicapped people.

However, it is part of the essence of the so-called 'village impulse' to want to be more than simply provisions for the mentally handicapped. The more the single person—handicapped or co-worker—steps out of the shadowy existence of a category into the light of the knowledge of his or her own singleness, and demands to be recognised in his or her uniqueness, the more the *social* consequences of such a knowledge develop. In this effort to understand the human being in his uniqueness, anthroposophy shows itself as today's supreme tool. No doubt future times will also be able to build on the fundamental insights of the first six lectures, which progress from the mask to the relationship to repeated earth lives, because the genius of the author Karl König has with sovereignty extended world understanding of anthroposophy. The transition in the last three lectures—from the personal to the social, from anthropology to the knowledge of man in its widest sense, from the learning–working image with its Christian centre to the threefold social organism—is a deed which will have to be recognised as the basis of any Christianised knowledge of man because it contains man not only in his individual constitution but man as a social being. Therefore the new organ which is spoken of in the second lecture of the third conference is not only an organ of new spiritual consciousness but is also an organ of a new social life.

This sudden widening from questions of the individual constitution to the social landscape of the fundamental social ordering of mankind is of special relevance today in view of contemporary trends and opinions. On the one hand there is the attempt in medicine, using foetal diagnostic techniques, to eradicate handicaps altogether; on the other hand there is the growing conviction that the remaining handicapped adults must be absorbed by society and not collected together in institutions, no matter how humane. But what society? The organisation of today's society is just not a reflection of the human organisation. Democracy, governmental party politics, voting, religious denominations, national boundaries, foreign policies, spying and so on, infinitely enhance the social loneliness of the individual, his social paralysis and unimportance.

In the beginning of the Camphill villages, the original founding co-workers strongly felt the importance of living together with the handicapped because in so doing a social edifice could be built that would be important not only as a provision for the handicapped person but for the wider establishment of a social order that is in keeping with the human condition and constitution.

The present tendency moves towards dividing men into those who are 'normal' and those who are not; the patients. The insight of the first lectures, starting with the masks, is of course a remarkable interpretation of the phenomenon of the handicapped adult: it is also a penetrating spiritual-scientific interpretation in the light of today's prejudices. Through widening this interpretation to encompass a social organism, an organism which must be *striven* for since it does not exist in the ideals of the past which underpin today's Western democracy, the thoughts of these lectures fire our enthusiasm and strengthen our will for the future.

Rev. Peter Roth O.B.E.
Botton Village,
January, 1986.

Contents

The Image of Man
as it pertains to our villagers

First Conference
held in Newton Dee Village, Aberdeen, Scotland.
9th–12th January 1962

Chairman's Opening Remarks

Peter Roth

Given on the evening of 9th January 1962

Dear Friends and dear Dr. König,

It is a wonderful thing that we can be here together for three days, after having lived for varying lengths of time through our manifold village experiences. These experiences were partly difficult, partly elevating, but time and again storm-tossed, windswept and painful because they were often clothed in a certain amount of darkness or of twilight. This conference takes place in order to combine these experiences and this search for an insight into how to live in our villages and how to acknowledge those human beings, the mentally handicapped, with whom we live. I feel that we have come together out of a great amount of darkness, wind and storm, and from many Camphill centres, to an island of peace and light. It may be that on this island of peace and light insights will gradually grow through our sharing of experiences and ideas, guided by Dr. König. Perhaps the darkness and the waves of the various village existences will, when we return to them, start to calm down.

I can imagine two reasons why the life and striving in the various villages is as it is. One is that the adolescents or adults with whom we live and work are still too little understood and recognised by us. It may be hoped that through the light shed by this conference we will be able not only to recognise them better but also to better shape our life and work around and with them. The other reason, I believe, is the following: that through the life in the villages, be they training centres or production places, the opportunity is given for one of the impulses of our time to incarnate a step further. This is the impulse of the threefold social organism. I can also imagine that this impulse of the threefold organism, which through the Camphill Movement has begun to incarnate somewhat, has found a new form of expression in the villages. Rudolf Steiner, when speaking about the inauguration of the future Michaelmas festival, referred to the Threefold Commonwealth impulse, which by that time had already been given up. He said that the propagation of this impulse, the attempt to carry it into the world, was something like a test of whether human souls would be worthy and strong enough to become true servants of Michael. This test had by then proved negative and Rudolf Steiner implied that therefore the outer manifestation of this impulse had to disappear. One could imagine that through the Camphill Movement in general, and the villages in particular, the impulse of the Threefold Commonwealth might find another foothold on the earth.

If in the course of these next three days we could find a connection between the people with whom we live and the threefold social organism, it would certainly be a very wonderful thing. You may remember that at the dedication of Botton Village, six and a half years ago, Dr. König's address closed with the thought that the outcasts of today are the forerunners of the future. That this holds good in our establishing of villages was implied by his words. It certainly shines through our windswept village existence and I hope it will lead to a certain amount of peace and light.

Perhaps the gods will incorporate our efforts into the rhythm of the extraordinary constellation which takes place at the beginning of February. During the night of February 4th/5th an eclipse of the sun will take place at which time Sun, Moon, Jupiter, Saturn, Mars, Venus and Mercury are all gathered within an angle of sixteen degrees. I feel that our conference may be worthily added to those impulses of this time that are offered to the spiritual world. This is a very wonderful thing.

Introduction

Karl König

Given immediately following the Chairman's Opening Remarks

Dear Friends,

It is certainly, as Peter said, a very wonderful thing that we have come together in order to clarify certain thoughts and to gain a certain amount of insight into the work which you are doing in the villages. It is quite amazing that it took more than seven years before such a thing came about. We should try, at the beginning of this meeting, to realise that a great deal of work, really a tremendous amount of work, has been done throughout the last seven years. Villages have been established, and seeds of villages have been sown as far away as America and South Africa; a beginning has also been made in Germany and Switzerland. Yet we did not come together to ask ourselves 'What are we actually doing?' or, 'How should we do it?'. Of course you have discussed this among yourselves; you have tried to formulate one or another thought. But now for the first time, from all parts of the Village Movement, friends have come together for no other purpose than to contemplate and meditate on what we are actually doing. This to me is very remarkable. It is as remarkable as a child who does not go to school directly he is born, but has to wait for seven years in order that the life of thought may begin to unfold in him in order to learn reading and writing.

It is my impression that we should now start together first of all to learn to distinguish the single letters of the village 'alphabet'. So far we are illiterate; we do not know, in truth, anything at all. We have toddled, we have played about, and in playing of course, nice things have begun to take shape. But now, we are told by our masters, school starts; and we make our first steps into Class I. We should realise that we are now to sit down, not in front of copy books or even text books, but we are to sit down and will have to learn first of all to make a straight line, then a curved line, and after that perhaps listen to a nice story that Peter will tell us, and then paint together or do a little bit of eurythmy—the first class. It is a pleasant experience if one has a good sense of humour; if not, it is not a nice experience!

We can, of course, ask who our teachers are. I don't know. It will transpire who they are and what they want of us. It will be a very condensed first class—three days only. Nevertheless we might carry away with us a certain amount of knowledge which we will have to use and to verify in our daily work. In this way I have the impression that this conference is something unique, because no attempt to work out the general ideas of village life for handicapped adults is known to me. So it is even an historic task which we are going to undertake. I don't think we should see this in too great a light. It will be a first attempt and it will be a modest attempt. But as an attempt it is of historic significance. We will see how far we get.

Let us concentrate on our task. Let us try to give every ounce of our inner strength to this effort, because it depends not only on those who speak, but also on those who listen—who carry what is said, who join in the discussion, who open up, who build this three days community—that revelation and insight may be gained. So I hope that we will come together, join our efforts, be open to this conference and its participants and thereby in the end we may be able to say we are grateful that we have been permitted to be together and gain new insight into our task.

First Lecture

Karl König

Given on the morning of 10th January 1962

Dear Friends,

As we now begin to consider our task during the next three days I have the impression that my contribution will be different from what you will bring out of your experience, because you have now lived for years together with those young men and women who are entrusted to you. You therefore have a certain amount, some of you even a wealth, of experience which I have not. I have never lived in either a village or a training centre except for occasional visits. I can therefore only bring to you something which is special, but which I am more or less convinced will be of some help to you, otherwise I would not take up your time. What we discuss together in the mornings will do nothing other than draw our attention to the conditions of those people who are within our care. What do we meet in them? My special question is not: 'What shall we do with them?' or, 'How shall we live together with them?' My question is: 'From which point of view can we learn to understand them?' And if I ask from which point of view can we learn to understand them, we already face a very great problem, dear friends. The problem is the following. Naturally, in the realm of curative work with children, it is quite obvious and quite necessary that we deal with the single child. Whether we are doctors or teachers, nurses or helpers, we meet in clinic or in case conference and we put the single child before us and try to understand him: try to understand the special destiny, the individuality, the shortcomings, the illness, of this particular single person. We all know this has proved invaluable for our work. We could even say that the individualisation, the special observation of the single child is one of the fundamentals of our life and of our work in the realm of special education.

However, as those who live with our villagers or pre-villagers know, (for the sake of our common understanding, permit me to call 'pre-villagers' those sixteen to eighteen year olds who are in our training centres, and 'villagers' those adults who live in our villages), in our life with the villagers we are in an entirely different position. Because we have all said to each other that it is no longer possible or even permissible for us to observe and to judge the individual person—not even to judge with the best possible intentions under the best possible conditions. If I say 'us', I exclude our doctors. Naturally the doctor's task is to judge; to diagnose the individual villager. There is no other choice: that is his job. But it is by no means ours. We are not in a position to look upon a grown-up person with whom we live, with whom we work, and with whom we share our life and destiny, in order to observe him and judge him as psychologists and doctors do. I think it would be fatal if we fell into this trap of modern life, because we would then become their gaolers and they would be our prisoners. We would lose at once the immediate human connection with them. We do not in the least have the right to look upon such a person in even the slightest way analytically—there is no justification by reason of our better intellect, our greater understanding, or our freer abilities with regard to our personality.*

But what are we to do? They are given into our charge; they are entrusted to us. But we cannot evade the point, dear friends, that there is a difference between our villagers and ourselves in certain spheres of existence. Yet in others there must be no difference. Excuse my pointing this out. I am aware that you know this very well, but if we want to go even one step further, it is necessary to build on this.

What is our task? As I understand it, dear friends, our task is to create in ourselves leading images—what in German we call *Leitbilder*—archetypal pictures. We should create in ourselves

---

* A statement by Rudolf Steiner that is relevant to this discussion is to be found in Appendix A.

archetypal pictures which begin more and more to live within us; pictures which in a general way begin to explain the existence of our villagers and help us understand their behaviour, their ways of reacting, their capabilities and their difficulties. These leading images, however, must remain within our soul, and must not be fitted, as it were, onto any single individual, so that we could say he is like this or she is like that. It can never be our task to pigeonhole the individual villager by means of these leading images. We must leave them entirely free; we must leave them as they are. But we must create in ourselves images of humanity. And these images of humanity live in us and gradually build up a mirror in which they, the villagers who are entrusted to us, can mirror themselves. They will not mirror themselves consciously of course, but unconsciously. If we carry such images within us, to the villagers they will subconsciously become the imprint of their own existence. They will give them step-by-step the possibility of understanding their own destiny on earth. I would propose that during the next three days we should try to understand and complete these leading images. This is my proposal. I will leave it with you.

However, there is something else, something which I feel is of the same importance as this first point, and it is the following. If you look at our villagers, if you meet them, if you deal with them, the question will arise: What do I really experience when I meet these men and women? What kind of common denominator holds good for all of them? You might give this or that answer which, in one or another way, will certainly be justified. But whenever I meet them, when I walk through the village or when I sit at table with them, I have gradually realised that here is something which begs to be understood. It is my impression that the common denominator which holds good for each of them is the following. I feel that whenever we meet them there is something hidden, but hidden in such a way that the individual destiny does not unfold as it does in the ordinary young person who at this age goes out into the world—whether the 'world' is work, school, university, job or whatever. Naturally every human being has a destiny which he has to fulfil here on earth during his life between birth and death. If he unfolds in an ordinary way, that is if he has gone through puberty, and has conquered puberty, he then enters step-by-step into the different spheres of his destiny. He thinks he is entering life, but in point of fact he enters nothing else but his own destiny, which he is going to fulfil in a more or less complete way. If this complete way is a very narrow one, it is his narrow destiny which he is going to fulfil. Do you understand the difference? An ordinary human being goes more or less fully through the wealth of his destiny, and for each one of us our destiny has a wealth of possibilities.

In our villagers destiny cannot fully unfold. With them only sections, perhaps just one, two or three sections of their destiny can be accomplished, because physical or other handicaps restrict the unfolding of their individuality. Their individuality is restricted, is kept in a certain confinement. Therefore, dear friends, every single one of them wears a mask. And one of the secrets of our work is the fact that we do not, immediately, meet the other individuality, but that between their individuality and our individuality there stands what I call a mask. Here (see diagram) are the individualities of our villagers, and there are the individualities of 'ordinary' people, (I try to avoid using the word 'normal'). Masks are put in front of them.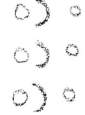

Don't think that we do not wear masks, dear friends, but our masks are different. Our masks are what kind of suit we wear; the way in which we get up in the morning, wash ourselves, clean our teeth, sit at the breakfast table, have porridge or cornflakes, tea or coffee. . . how our rooms are furnished, whether we are in need or the opposite of need, and so on. These are our masks, but they are differentiated masks; the individualised masks of our personal habits. The masks of our villagers are general masks; their masks are 'masks of humanity'.

What do I mean by this? You see, if you have ever been to a *Carnival* in Basel or in one of the cities of the Rhineland, or wherever *Carnival* still has a certain tradition, for days on end you will meet people wearing masks. And if you ask yourself 'What are they wearing?' you will come to understand that they are hiding their individual face behind a generalized mask: caricatures of humanity, animal masks, devil masks and so on. The Greek actor, for instance, had to wear a mask because he was portraying not an individual, but a type of humanity. If you observe, for instance, the dances of primitive peoples, you will notice how masks of lions or tigers, bears and so on are worn, how the whole body is clad in something entirely foreign to it, and you will suddenly realise that they are enacting a being which is not their own individuality, but to which their individuality is utterly given up, and thus something entirely new is present.

Our villagers have to wear such 'masks of humanity'. This, dear friends, is their task in life which they have to live. Therefore the leading images (*Leitbilder*) which we have to gradually evolve, to build, to model within our soul; these archetypal pictures will be 'masks of humanity'. So, in building up these images within us, we will walk among our villagers knowing what they do not know: but not looking at the mask and saying to ourselves he is wearing this or she is wearing that mask. It is part of our task—I would like to say our holy task—that we keep this within the secret cell of our existence. And only in this way will we be able to leave them, our villager friends who are entrusted to us, free to recognise themselves if they wish to do so; if their destiny, if their angel wishes them to do so. We have no right to recognise them. But it is our task to carry within us these 'masks of humanity' in order that they have the opportunity, I repeat dear friends, in order that they have the opportunity to look into these masks if they wish to do so.

But our first and foremost endeavour is that under no circumstances are we to judge them. It is not for us to understand them as individuals; it is for us to give them the possibility to understand themselves. Can you see the difference between the doctor and us? I have the impression that these are the basics which, first and foremost, we have to learn to respect. This is the self-education which we have to undergo; the self-discipline not to say: Sarah is such and such, this is her I.Q., and therefore I will give her this or that task. You are already wrong to do so. When such a human being is assigned to one of our places, we have to find where they should live and work, but according to the needs of the village almost without regard to the individuality. Dear friends, can you understand that? *According to the needs of the village*, they must be placed according to the needs of housing space. It is somewhat different with the pre-villagers: as trainees they occupy a position between school and village life. We shall speak about them in a moment. For the villagers, however, this is, I think, the only acceptable attitude toward them. As soon as one begins to interview an applicant, to look into his handwriting, to have it tested, to let him go through tests at all, one restricts the freedom of the human being entirely. I think one cannot do anything worse, even if one is a psychologist, than to test people.

These are the first fundamentals, more or less, which we must now learn to understand. As I said, there is naturally a difference between the pre-villagers and the villagers. The pre-villagers, and I will speak about them now, come to us when they are sixteen, seventeen or eighteen years old, still in the process of puberty. In order to understand them we have to learn about the pubescent process. None of these masks, dear friends, was present during childhood. The child, the school-child, is still an individual. He usually still has all the possibilities of fulfilling his destiny; the world is at his feet. But this changes as soon as puberty arrives. The individuality which was appearing need not continue to unfold. With many of our children (not all, of course, but with many) during the process of puberty something special turns into something general; something individual turns into a mask. Now it is quite clear that every boy or girl that is going through puberty takes on something of the 'mask of humanity'. We are quite wrong in thinking that it is just through puberty that we become individuals. On the contrary, just through puberty we lose our individuality to a certain extent, and regain it only gradually when we become nineteen, twenty or twenty-one years of age. Then something begins to shine through which in the course of the next twenty years starts to unfold as the individuality. Don't think that you are a personality when you are thirty; you are still in the throes of the 'mask of humanity'. There is no other choice, dear friends. Only at around forty do you start to become, do you even have the possibility of becoming, an individual.

Rudolf Steiner has given us the image of the development of the child and the young person in a fundamental way. (Dr. König draws on the blackboard.) Here is birth, and the first seven year period; then the second seven year period, and here would be puberty.

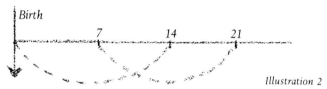

Illustration 2

Then the third seven year period follows and this would be the twenty-first year. We also know, at least to a certain extent we think we know, that during these three seven year periods fundamental steps of development are made. We develop our physical body during the first period, our ether body during the second period, our astral body during the third period—and here our ego, our individuality, begins to shine through. We begin the steps into our destiny.

Under no circumstances would it be justified to say that these nodal points of birth, the changing of teeth, puberty and full maturity are periods of change that in themselves are similar or equal. Quite the opposite is the case. Because if you begin to evaluate these four focal points of our development during childhood and youth, you will come to appreciate that the step at seven years can only be compared with the step at twenty-one years and that birth is comparable to puberty. You will soon understand what I mean. With regard to birth, the body begins to appear. And we are all born entirely sick.* There is no child who is not, from the point of view of humanity, a sick person. And the first seven years are nothing other than the gradual overcoming of the sickness of birth. I mean this very seriously. The sickness of being thrown into this world, thrown bodily into this world, is, so to speak, the repetition of the Fall. The physical fall into sinfulness; this is what happens during our birth. Only because our common ideas and

---

* For a further understanding of this statement it might be helpful to regard the newborn as ill-adapted to the environment through the undeveloped physical condition; equally at puberty there is ill-adaptation of the newly awakening soul powers which as yet lack experience and mature judgement.

concepts are so poorly formed do we look at a little baby as if it were the healthiest possible thing on earth. In fact it is a most sick being. Therefore the death rate in babies is the highest of all stages of life. We are all born sick. But I don't mean this in the sense of Savonarola, dear friends. Birth is nothing else than a process of sickness; and we gradually rise, as it were, to a certain degree of health. With the seventh year we have advanced to a certain harmony with regard to our health. Therefore Rudolf Steiner quite rightly says the second seven year period is the healthiest period of our life. Any Medical Officer will tell you that the lowest rate of death occurs between the seventh and fourteenth year (except accidents on the road; these road accidents are the killers, but this is not through the illness of the child but through the illness of the civilisation). And now, you see, beginning with the twelfth year a decline sets in and puberty is again a fall into sickness. Only gradually, by the twenty-first year, do we start to regain our health—and it takes until death for us to be fully restored.

This is a new way of looking at our life. But it is a true, a very true way. And what we have to deal with when we live with the pre-villagers is the following. You see here birth and puberty (see drawing) and you will immediately understand what I mean if I say that in birth we are born into the world bodily, whereas with puberty we are born into the world with regard to our soul and our spiritual being. Rudolf Steiner describes how during the fourteenth, fifteenth and sixteenth year man is released from out of the Spirit. It is the second Fall through which we go.

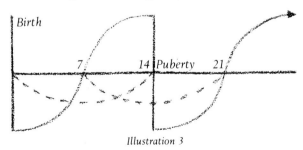

Illustration 3

And being released out of the Spirit—bumping against a hard world physically, a world full of destiny—brings about a change which every young person suffers during this age. The soul and spirit, naked to begin with, meet the world. Here (pointing to the drawing) the body has to regain its health. Here the soul and spirit have to regain their health and adjustment. These are general terms, dear friends. We will not make more specific ones.

We want to understand puberty because some of our centres have to deal with the young people, pre-villagers, who are still in the throes of the process of puberty. I would like to remind you of what we have begun to work through in Camphill when two years ago we occupied ourselves with the seven life processes of which Rudolf Steiner spoke. You will permit me to write them down in German, and I will then translate the seven words which Rudolf Steiner uses, because it is not easy to give the same meaning in English which is assigned to them in German. Rudolf Steiner describes the seven life processes as follows: *Atmung, Wärmung, Ernährung, Absonderung, Erhaltung, Wachstum* and *Regeneration.*[1]

Atmung: In- and exhaling between Man and World

Wärmung: Warming

Ernährung: Nourishing

Absonderung: Secreting

Erhaltung: Maintaining

Wachstum: Growing

Regeneration: Reproducing

In this connection, *Atmung* does not only mean ordinary breathing, in the element of air, but the totality of exchange between the world and our bodily nature. The inhaling and exhaling which plays between world and self is what is meant, but as a general, an immense, a vast all-breathing process, when Rudolf Steiner puts it as the first of the seven life processes. This inhaling and exhaling has to be kept together as the next step so that the exhaling does not disappear, and the inhaling does not harden in itself. It has to go through the process of warming. The warming process is a permeating mantle which keeps inhaling and exhaling together, and thereby the sphere of an organism is created. This is something which communicates with the world but remains nonetheless itself; communicates by breathing with the world, but remains itself through a mantle of warmth. This is now the space of a living existence. But now, going one step lower, it acquires *Ernährung*—we can say 'nourishment'. It begins to take in substances which it does not immediately mix up (as in inhaling and exhaling), but which it keeps and then destroys. It can only keep and destroy by immediately developing something of the next process, which is 'secreting'. In secreting, the inner part meets the outer, the nourishing part, and these two work together. The saliva and all the secretions we produce in stomach and intestine—all this meets the food we take in, breaks it down, and gradually step-by-step transforms it into ourselves. This is the process of 'maintaining'. Now we begin to substantially maintain this organism, the sphere of which was built by the first two processes. So at first we had the building of a sphere; now with nourishing, secreting and maintaining the sphere is filled with substance. This is not difficult to understand so far, is it? And at last what has been filled—and is now maintaining itself—begins to sprout. We have the process of growing and also the process of reproducing. However, reproducing does not only mean the begetting of offspring: we continually have to reproduce ourselves. We have to regenerate our body, otherwise we would not exist. Because we continually shed bodily substance, through urine and skin and hair and nails, everything goes, and we have to regenerate it. Only part of this reproductive process is the begetting of offspring. These are all the preliminaries, dear friends, and please remember that we are only in the forecourt of the kindergarten.

Rudolf Steiner describes that through the Fall of Man these seven life processes have changed. (Again permit me to write down the German words, because they are better coined than the English ones). Breathing or *Atmung* becomes *Verbrauchen*. *Wärmung* turns into *Verbrennen*. *Ernährung* becomes *Ablagerung*. *Absonderung* remains unchanged; this central part remains unchanged. But *Erhaltung* becomes *Verhärtung; Wachstum* turns into *Reifung; Regeneration* turns into *Generation*. I have tried to work out a possible translation. *Verbrauchen* is Consuming. *Verbrennen* is Burning or Combustion.

Ablagerung is Depositing. *Verhärtung* is Sclerosis. *Reifung* is Maturing or Maturation. *Generation* is Generation or Reproduction. I will try to explain what it all means.

Atmung (Breathing) — *Verbrauchen* (Consuming)

Wärmung (Warming) — *Verbrennen* (Burning)

Ernährung (Nourishing) — *Ablagerung* (Depositing)

Absonderung (Secreting) —

Erhaltung (Maintaining) — *Verhärtung* (Sclerosis)

Wachstum (Growing) — *Reifung* (Maturing)

Regeneration (Regeneration) — *Generation* (Reproduction)

What is meant by breathing turning into consuming? The free exchange of inhaling and exhaling no longer flows through an organism and thereby carries the organism with it, but breathing is taken hold of, and substances like oxygen are used up. Can you see this difference? Instead of inhaling and exhaling, the assimilatory and dissimilatory process begins. Burning: warming turns into burning— which also means that warmth turns into fire. Fire now burns within the body and consumes substances; consumes the oxygen inhaled with the air. The process thereby becomes egoistic. Nourishing: this causes substances not only to be taken in and exchanged, but also to be deposited; deposited, for instance, as gallstones, as urine, as brain substance, as liver substance: deposited in every conceivable way. It is assimilated. It is deposited.

If you ponder over this, the question will arise: When does this change take place in our life? Dear friends, it happens the moment we are born, therefore our birth is sick. You see, as an embryo, as a foetus, we rest in the motherly womb. There, breathing is not consuming; warming is not burning; nourishing is not depositing. The life processes unfold according to cosmic images and cosmic principles. But when we are born and pushed into this world, everything in us begins to be consumed, to be burned, to be deposited. When Rudolf Steiner gave these indications he described this change as coming about through Ahriman.

If you look at the next process, in which maintaining turns into sclerosis, this means nothing else than that death sets in. Naturally, even at the gate of birth death is setting in, only now this happens in a more apparent manner. Our body begins to calcify, to become sclerotic, to become old. Growing is no longer growing like a plant, growing without an end, without an aim, like the birds' singing— growing in the way that children below the age of puberty grow. As soon as puberty sets in growing turns into maturing, into maturation. In the boy the larynx now sclerotizes; his voice turns deep. In the girl the breasts start to grow, the whole body becomes ripe, and yet still maintains a high rate of growth. But this growing is now a ripening process, so that at roughly about the twentieth year growth comes to an end because we have become ripe. And with regard to reproducing, we no longer reproduce our own body; as a result of the ripening process, we are also gradually able to reproduce our own offspring. When Rudolf Steiner gave these indications he said these three processes are under the impact and influence of Lucifer.

So here (see drawing) you have the process of birth, and here you have the process of puberty. And now you will understand why I made this fundamental distinction between the seventh and twenty-first year on the one hand and birth and puberty on the other. We deal with sclerosis, maturation and reproduction when we have to deal with young people after puberty; this is the mask which they put on. Every one! But our villagers are masked in a much greater, more profound way, than any ordinary young person at this age. You may remember an instance when you had not seen a child of thirteen or fourteen for some months, and then when you see him again you stand in front of him flabbergasted. Is he the same? What has happened to him? What has taken place? Who is he? And don't think he has now become the expression of his personality, of his individuality. He is now the expression of the 'mask of humanity', which we now have to learn to deal with. We have to try on the one hand not to let the personality entirely drown behind the mask, and I don't mean only the mask in front of the face; I mean the mask all round. On the other hand we have to learn to deal with the mask itself.

This is as far as I wanted to go this morning.

Discussions with Dr. König

Question. Can the mask be seen as arising from the temperaments?

Dr. König. Very interesting! In a sense it is definitely in the same realm, though the realm of the mask is much wider still than that of the temperaments. If it is possible for us to meet again in a year or two, we will discover that the mask is in reality everything that Jung was after when he described the Archetypes. The Archetypes in point of fact are the masks.

Comment. When you described the transformation of the life processes from the cosmic into the earthly, one might think that the hardening and sclerosis are connected with Ahrimanic influences rather than Lucerific ones.

Dr. König. One might, but one should not. It is not necessary. Sclerosis, maturing, procreation are the result of Lucifer. Suppose you are very Lucerific and inclined to drink a good deal of alcohol, the result will be sclerosis of the liver.

Question. The masks are very complicated, giving rise to complicated thoughts. Can one talk about the mask of anger, or the mask of old age? Where do etheric and astral influences finish and individuality express itself without the mask?

Dr. König. I consider the mask as something we wear continually. But also we continually break through the mask—and as ordinary people we put on different masks at different times; at different hours, even at different minutes. Our handicapped friends have only a few masks at their disposal and they do not have the freedom to break through their mask, put it down, or put on another one. Not that we have this fully within our freedom either. We have acquired our set of masks, for example, the mask of the one who gets up in the morning, which after a time is laid down and another is taken up. We have the masks of positivity, of receptivity, the mask of the listener to music, the mask of the representative of God, the mask of the father, the brother, the uncle, the sister, the player, the lover, the husbandman, the sower, the shepherd: without masks we are unable to follow the path of our existence. Waldorf education enables people to wear as many masks as possible, whereas our handicapped friends wear only two, three or four masks; therefore their destiny is narrowed down. Our masks are so numerous and varied that we continually mirror ourselves in the various conditions of our existence. We can adjust ourselves.

An animal wears one mask only. He is for instance a lion and he will never be able to escape this. If he did not remain a lion, he would not be able to remain part of the animal group soul; with the mask of the lion he represents his higher being. Only in childhood does the lion wear more than one mask, when he is still playing—I say 'he' consciously—and has not yet become a father lion, a mother lion, a hunter lion. Also a young monkey playing about still wears different masks—even at times human masks—but when he grows up all this comes to an end. And so it is with the stagnation in our young friends—this is their mask. They have adjusted themselves to the life in the village. Take them out and it will be very difficult for them. This is not to say anything against the village people, but we have to learn to recognise this.

Question. From what I observe in our villages there is a kind of theatrical quality about our villagers. One can say that all life is a stage, but in our village this seems to be literally true, more so than elsewhere. No doubt this is linked with the wearing of masks as has been described. But why is it necessary that human beings hide behind a mask at all, and why are our young friends more of a mask than others? Why is it much more difficult for them to break through the mask than it is for us?

Question. Can masks be found also in the realm of the spiritual hierarchies, or only in the sphere of the *Urbilder* (Archetypes)? Do Lucifer and Ahriman wear masks?

Dr. König. Throughout the whole of the spiritual world, in so far as the spiritual world presents itself in the disguise which is the mask of substance. You even find masks in the ether.

Comment. I would like to put the question in different words. I feel that the masks which we wear simply have the advantage that our individuality can be manifold. Through the manifoldness of the mask we can, to an extent, overcome the process of hardening, of sclerosis.

Dr. König. So that sclerosis does not overcome us; we are able to balance it.

Question. When other people meet our villagers, especially those who have been in our care for a long time, they often express the feeling of having met something special. We ourselves may frequently experience the individuality to a greater extent than one would expect. The question now is, what touches us when we meet these youngsters? Is it perhaps the discrepancy between the mask and the enshrined individuality? Is it their inherent possibility of wearing manifold masks—and then the confession of our own failure when we have to acknowledge that they have been able to develop only a very few masks? Perhaps we would have to say that if they had not been with us they would have fewer masks still; that with us they have acquired some more. One might ask oneself: 'Why does a mother put them into this garment?' Maybe she has an image which she does not want them to find. I am thinking of the story of Parsifal and the fool's garments his mother put on him.

Dr. König. It is a lovely image.

Question. In certain situations we meet our young people and we say 'They were truly themselves', for example during the Sunday service. Do we now mean that the individuality is shining through, or that we have succeeded in giving them another mask? Two scenes come to my mind from the Old Testament—one most beautiful scene where Jacob at last meets his brother Esau, and he says "Thy face is as the face of God!". And there is another passage where Moses is referred to and it says "He wist not that the skin of his face shone."

Comment. There are, of course, very many people who are not in our villages, who are in the world, having in their possession a rather small number of masks—but they use them in the right place—the mask of the churchgoer, the mask of the father or the mask of the craftsman.

Dr. König. These are the masks which one calls the masks of well adjusted people.

Comment. The difficulty only appears if the mask is in the wrong place—for instance the father is in the workshop, the churchgoer at home. Maybe it does not only depend on the number of masks, but rather that the right one is worn at the right time.

Dr. König. What makes our young people so mask-like is their inability to wear the right mask in the right place. They have, for instance, the mask of the craftsman, but with this they also eat and attend a service—and everything remains the same, until perhaps another mask is put on, say a hymn-singing mask. This we have also to learn to see.

I am well aware that if I speak of the mask I am saying something which to all intents and purposes is very dangerous, and I would beg you not to expound this in any way to the world. For years and years I did not dare to speak about the mask, although I have seen it very clearly. However I have the impression that we must learn to understand it, but we must treat such an idea very carefully—and we are never to forget that behind each mask in every human being there stands an individuality. It is also not a question of whether the mask is to be torn down, because here on earth we have to wear a mask. Even our physical-etheric-astral body is the mask of our previous incarnations. This does not inhibit the individuality; it helps the individuality. It is the rungs of the ladder on which the individuality climbs higher. The mask can be the friend or foe of the individuality, but the mask is something that has to be there. I am convinced, however, that if, during a service for instance, you meet the individuality, it is not another mask. The individuality shines through, permeates the mask. Any mask can be permeated, as with Moses when his skin shone. It is a threefold experience, but usually all three aspects are together. The first experience is one of wonder, of awe and wonder. We experience awe and wonder in the face of the fact that a mask is there, because only seldom does a mask shine undisturbed by the personality. Through this we meet some kind of archetypal image which otherwise is personalised. In our handicapped friends we meet, for instance, the perfect shepherd; or we meet the perfect eater; or we meet the perfect churchgoer. This is the one thing. The second experience is one of compassion in the face of the discrepancy between masks and individuality. We experience that whatever we do, there is always the mask and the individuality; and the two clash. We hope that some time the two will come together. The third experience is the immediate concern of our conscience to meet the individuality behind the mask. This is the threefold experience merged into one. If you permit me to say it like this, it is the trinity of experience when we meet our handicapped friends.

Question. I wondered in which way the *Leitbild*—this image which we should carry with us—is related to the mask?

Dr. König. The masks should be recognised by us, and these masks are the images—the *Leitbilder*—which we have to carry with us. Tomorrow we will learn to recognise two masks, and the day after tomorrow three masks. And gradually you will learn, in the course of the coming year, to recognise many more masks; the shepherd, the churchgoer, the father, the mother, and so on. But we will have to learn the relative importance of a mask so that we know which ones we have especially to build up in our souls—so that they can be a mirror we carry for our handicapped friends to see themselves in. It is not for us to judge. If a shepherd comes to us, he does not necessarily have to tend the sheep. He can also work with the cows, or in the weaving shop or wherever. Thereby his destiny is widened. If we only make him a shepherd we would hinder his development.

Comment. Some years back, Thomas* urged us to make use of the abilities of those who are growing older, by incorporating them into a working process. Perhaps it was only I who made the mistake that again and again we adopted a 'curative educational' point of view rather than a 'village' point of view. We have to establish someone in his ability from a social work point of view and also from a village therapeutic point of view. This means that we arrange the life in such a way that he is enabled to wear his mask at the right moment. It means that we adjust the surroundings to meet his needs—and in guiding him rightly we hope and try very hard to ensure that the adjustment which we have helped him make will in course of time enable him to increase his possibility to adjust to other surroundings also. There is a subtle difference in the approach; one must not continue a curative educational approach beyond the walls of the schools.

Dr. König. The knowledge of the mask remains within us. It should be our rule not to use the mask in an individual but only in a general way. Let them wear their masks. We should react to them as if we did not recognise them, except within ourselves. But this recognition should have no outward results, or they are unable to become active themselves. If we put them in the place where we want them put, we restrict their freedom, we restrain their abilities. It is the same as if we would give them a tranquilizer . . . well, there is perhaps a slight difference. We clamp down on something, when really we have to make their individuality expand. We should give up the idea of making things as easy as possible, because then we take away this potential for growing.

Comment. I have met the criticism from the side of the authorities that we run the risk of making things too easy for the young people,

---

* Dr. Thomas J. Weihs, Medical Officer of the Camphill Schools.

which does not help what they call rehabilitation into the wider community outside. When we listen to what they have to say, they feel inclined to respond: 'All well and good, but you don't adjust them to life outside.'

Dr. König. They are the ones who make it so easy for the human being to become just a robot. And there we should speak out very clearly.

Comment. It is an extraordinary thing that the working mask can be imposed on the handicapped person successfully. But the moment the factory gate is shut behind them there is a void. Then they have no other masks to wear. To approach the handicapped person with awe, compassion and conscience is the only alternative. I can imagine that this, in some appropriate way, could also be understandable for outer knowledge, outer science. Because the moment one has awe, one is able to distinguish the mask from the individuality, at the same time giving the mask its due.

Dr. König. I would be grateful if tomorrow we could have the picture 'Light and Shadow' here, and the day after tomorrow Rudolf Steiner's sketch of 'Threefold Man'. Perhaps we could have it in a frame for the occasion.

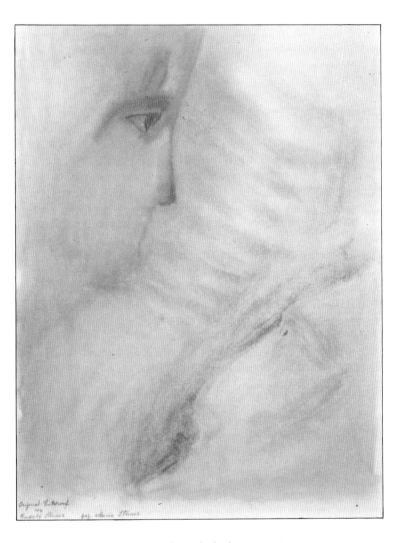

Light and Shadow
Rudolf Steiner

Second Lecture

Karl König

Given on the morning of 11th January 1962

Dear Friends,

We will begin where we left off yesterday morning, but we may have to retrace our steps even further, because it is so important that during these three days we reach—or rather, reach out for—the right points of view. So much of our work during the coming year will depend on whether we are able to start from a correct point of view. This will be necessary because when we began to concieve the idea of this conference we did so in the hope of gradually establishing a training course for people who would prefer to work in our villages instead of working with handicapped children in our schools. We are very far from being able to start such a training course, very far indeed. And it is also unlikely, dear friends, that three, four, ten or even twenty lectures will make possible the start of such a training course.

But if we gain the right points of view today, and if you earnestly take up these points of view as indications—if about twenty or thirty of you begin to develop these indications—then within a year we may be one or even two steps further. Many different opportunities for many new points of view will emerge, and out of this a certain wealth of ordered experience will be streaming into one vessel. And if this ordered experience is then shaped we might be able to say: 'Now we know what subjects we will have to teach in such a training course'. The Camphill training course in Curative Education only started in 1949. So it took nine years; and even then it was very humble; a very modest beginning. Yet it started. And time and again you will have to remind one another that you must gradually learn to order your experiences because, dear friends, so far within your work you were as little children. You were simply playing and toddling about, trying to manage as well as you could. I would even go so far as to say that all of us in the village movement were like the 'Rider over the Lake of Constance'[2] who crossed the lake on horseback without knowing that he was crossing a frozen lake and that the ice might have given way at any moment. It is my impression that we have reached the shore, but we should not react as the rider did when he realised the danger he had been in. He was suddenly so shocked that he dropped down dead. This would be the wrong reaction on our part!

I would like to make the point once more that we must begin from the infant stage and develop into school life. But we should go into our own school, which means we should start to learn from our own experiences, from everyday life, to be able to observe our own reactions. It will be most important that we begin to understand the special inner life which people will have to lead who live in a village—those who work with adult handicapped men and women. We must take this very seriously. Our inner development will, of course, be an individual one, and no doubt nothing will interfere with this. But we will definitely have to learn that gradually a certain amount of inner education must be found for our special life in the villages and in the training centres. If, for instance, you start to occupy yourself with the problem of the mask to which I referred yesterday—not merely to read what I said, but to take it up actively as an inner exercise and observe in your daily life what the mask is— then more and more you will begin to make the first steps in this special direction of becoming a responsible person in the work of our villages.

You see, dear friends, when we walk among our young handicapped friends we increasingly learn to observe that each one is what in everyday language we would call a 'character'. No one of us is so markedly a 'character' as are our young friends. Would you agree? They are 'characters' in the true sense of the word. And their being a 'character' is much more 'juicy', much more flesh and blood than any of us. In point of fact, if we look at each other, (all those of you here in this room are of course excepted!) but generally if we look at ourselves, with few exceptions we are more or less shadows of existence in comparison with those who are such full-blooded characters. Nothing disturbs them, but anything can disturb us. Whenever there is an unusual situation they will remain unshakeably who they are. We, however, are definitely thrown out of gear if a train is late or a telephone does not function, if the stove goes out or the hot water is not running. All this is unbearable for us, because we are such shadow existences that we depend on these gadgets. But for these characters, even if the sun were not to rise one morning they would remain what they are, firmly implanted into existence.

If we ask ourselves why this is so, dear friends, naturally we may all see this from many different points of view. But what makes them 'characters' is no doubt connected with their being masks. They are masks which are not easily disturbed. To be either a mask or to unmask continually is the difference which I want to point out. In their mask-appearance they are simply representatives of the astral forces of the world and of their own astral forces. I could even say 'mask' and 'astrality' are identical, only you should not write it down in the form of a mathematical equation. But to be a mask means to have a formed-out astral body; and this astral body represents—and don't misunderstand me, dear friends—this astral body represents an ego. Don't mistake it for the individual; don't mistake it for *the* ego. The full-bloodedness of their mask existence is their astrality, which can appear in many different ways. Our shadow existence in comparison with theirs is the beginning of the appearance of our individuality: our ego is gradually peeping through, peering out, and what we see is nakedness.

You remember, for instance, how time and again Rudolf Steiner pointed out the fact that our ego, compared with our other members, is a baby. This is because it is a beginning. When living among our younger and older handicapped friends we have to learn to understand and to evaluate their and our existences, together with our differences. Then we discover that, compared with them, we are the babies whether we like it or not. Therefore I have so often heard it said: 'They are doing this for our sake; without them we could not do it.' Indeed, we could not. You see, during the last hundred years the world has plunged into mechanisation, ordering the outer framework of life for this little nothingness which is breaking through as the human individuality, the human ego. As long as people lived in their sentient soul, the ego was embedded in the cradle of the soul. When people began to live in the mind soul the ego still lived in the cradle of the soul, the bed of astrality. Millions, even hundreds of millions still live in the intellectual or mind soul today. All the eastern peoples, Czechs, Finns, Hungarians, Russians—they all live in the mind soul, the *Gemüts und Verstandesseele*. Only special people like the Anglo-Americans, the Westerners, begin to unmask at times. Their individuality, their ego, begins to peep through the mask. We have to recognise this first of all, but to recognise it by daily inner effort.

You see if you now go to school, or decide to start to go to school, (I can only suggest this to you; it remains up to you whether or not you accept it), then you must make clear every morning, without fail, that today you are going to find out the difference between the revelations of astrality and the signs and symptoms of the ego. Only then will you begin to refine your inner observations to such an extent that our young friends will not only be your helpers, but that you will begin to provide them with your inner help: you from within, they from without. This would be an excellent co-operation. But it will only begin to happen if you not only listen attentively to what I say now, but if you also decide: 'From tomorrow on, I will take off the jacket of my habits and start every morning to attempt this differentiation.' That is the first point. I hope you don't mind if I speak like this because it really is 'either/or'. The second point is the following. If you want to graduate in this work you will have to take up a certain amount of study, and I would advise you to study something very special; something which a few of you have already begun to study, but which many of you have missed and thereby missed a tremendous amount of life, joy and experience. You see, dear friends, because we are all of us such shadow-existences, we lack a great deal of life-experience: experience of the tremendous diversity of human existence. Certainly, those of us who have worked in our curative schools have seen it in the children, and we have experienced it when we met the parents. But the immense richness and variety of characters who walk about in this world, (they were once especially noticeable in British towns), can no longer be experienced because the consciousness soul is on its way. However, we can replace this because during the last century there were a number of heroes—heroes of spirituality, heroes of humanity—who gathered together in the richness of their own soul an immensity of inner existence as images of men, images of humanity. They were the great writers of the last century, who wrote the great novels which a few of you know but which many of you have never taken to reading. I refer here, for instance, to a man like Charles Dickens. Nothing would enhance your knowledge of characters more than the immense differences of fully-formed astralities that are described in *David Copperfield* or *The Pickwick Papers* or, indeed, in any of his novels. Of course you will say: 'When do we have the time to read? We have to do housework . . .' But one such novel every two or three months is quite enough, instead of reading any of these modern novels. If you read novels by Thomas Mann you have nothing to hold in your hands after you have turned the last page, whereas after you have read Tolstoy or Victor Hugo for instance, you have something to put into the pocket of your existence: children and characters and hunchbacks and giants. You can carry these within you and you will discover that they are exactly like our friends. I will mention a few more names. Besides Dickens, Tolstoy, and Victor Hugo you can read Thackeray and the Brontës, W. Rabe, Fontane, Pushkin, Balzac and Turgenjeff, Soloviev, J. Wassermann, C.F. Meyer, Selma Lagerlöf, Sigrid Undset, and Zola. Reading this is full of joy—it does not matter if perhaps it is not very agreeable; you simply take a plunge into astrality, which is necessary if you want to learn to understand the difference between astrality and ego. There are still a few, even right into our own time, who are great novelists in this sense. We can make up for our own lack of experience by the tremendous variety and manifoldness of human beings depicted in these novels. You would not be able to replace it, dear friends, by Shakespeare; it is something entirely different. He does not describe characters but types of men, and this is not what I mean; I mean life experience. I am not saying anything against Shakespeare, only that in this respect he would not be able to provide what Dickens, Thackeray and Tolstoy are able to give you.

Nor, please, Walter Scott; his novels are useless in this respect, absolutely useless, because I do not consider you teenagers any more.

Something else should also be taken up in this connection. (I provide you now with a kind of curriculum). I could well imagine that this could become a first step in your so-called 'College Meetings'. You could, for instance, make it your task to discuss figures from a novel of this type. And *the* novel *par excellence* for our purpose is Goethe's *Wilhelm Meister*. There is nothing which is so beautiful, and in itself so full of life, as this. All the other novels I mentioned are nothing else but variations. I don't mean *Wanderjahre* (Journeyman) but *Lehrjahre* (Apprentice). Had this book not been written, the others would not have followed, because here is an archetypal image. Occupy yourself with this archetypal image. Take up a person like Jago; the one who went to America and then came back again. There are at least twenty or thirty archetypal images of humanity which will help you to form your own inner images. Out of these *Leitbilder*, these leading images, you will then gradually be able to see the variations. But I must warn you of one thing very earnestly, dear friends. A few of you, especially the leading ones, might now think: 'Oh we will study the history of the novel; how novels developed through the sixteenth, seventeenth and eighteenth centuries. We will unravel the spiritual history exactly'. Don't do this, please. It might be a very interesting individual study, but it would be better to read *Wuthering Heights* than *History of the Novel*. Among German anthroposophists a story is told how after the crumbling earth existence has gone into pralaya the souls appear again and amongst them are many leading anthroposophists. Now there are two road signs in the spiritual world—one says 'To Jupiter' and the other says 'To a lecture on Jupiter'. And of course here the division starts. The anthroposophists go to the lecture, the ordinary people go towards Jupiter. I would advise you to go to Jupiter; I mean read the novels and don't go to a lecture on novels.

After this piece of self-education we will now return to the point where yesterday morning we spoke about puberty. We were able to understand how the three life-forces:

growing — maintaining — generating

were turned through Lucerific influences into:

maturation — scleroticizing — sexual propagation.

These three brought on puberty, and with this process the human soul, the human astrality, is born into this physical world; born into this world as fourteen years previously the physical body had been. With the birth of the astral body something immediately appears which manifests as the twofoldness of the Male and the Female. I know that also before this occurs there are boys and girls, but it is not yet a twofoldness because each boy has a tremendous amount of girlish qualities and vice versa. If you remember any child of nine, ten or eleven years of age, he or she is still not properly either male or female, though certain qualities point either to the one direction or the other. The general type of humanity stands out much more in this second seven year period of development. But the moment puberty begins, when it has started to set in, the male character and the female character stand out very clearly. And this twofoldness is one of the first things which you are called upon to observe. As you begin to develop an inner, refined feeling for what is male and what is female, you will immediately be able to go about the world establishing order in the surroundings. There are wonderful indications by Rudolf Steiner about this, and I would like to read a few to you. The first is from a lecture which Rudolf Steiner gave on the 4th of January 1922, in the educational course held in Dornach at Christmas 1921 and on into January 1922.[3] There he says:

> The woman bears the fullness of humanity within her, as does the man, but in such a way that she perceives it as a gift from other worlds; as something that has literally poured into the world from the heavens. The woman sees mankind in such a way that she has a picture—albeit an unconscious one, a background image as it were—according to which her idea of mankind is formed. The woman regards mankind primarily from the basis of moral values. She evaluates, she assesses.

In comparison to this Rudolf Steiner says:

> The man bears humanity in his inner being in such a way
> that he experiences the human being as a riddle, as
> something which he cannot completely comprehend; that
> poses him inexpressibly profound questions with which he
> cannot fully come to terms.

You see the twofoldness. The woman in her inner life has an all-round image of mankind. She carries this image and is more or less satisfied with it as long as she is able to judge it by a standard: her own standard, and her own values. Therefore the woman is the one who can bear the children, because it is in connection with this image which the woman has of the fall of mankind that the image of the child arises in her womb. You understand that this is not a conscious process; it lies in the unconscious and only at times peeps through into consciousness. This is as it were the condition in which the woman ought to stand in the world. The man, on the other hand, is continually tortured by questions. Humanity confronts him as a riddle and he wants to solve it; he never accepts it. He wants to solve it, to understand it, and ever and again new questions arise.

As soon as our boys and girls reach maturity, we immediately meet this problem in every possible variation and distortion. You can see so many of our young men being tortured, and simply falling into distress, giving up the possibility of solving the enigma, and thereby taking on a mask. I can think of a number of them in the village, a great number. On the other hand I know of a great number of the women-folk who have accepted, who evaluate, even if their evaluation is according to a very small measure. But this does not matter; what matters is that it is there. To develop a feeling for such differences is very important.

Rudolf Steiner gives another indication, in which he says:

> Love is therefore something totally different in man and in
> woman. In the woman love originates in her imaginative
> fantasy and is always connected with the forming of an
> image. The woman—please forgive me for saying this—
> never just loves the real man as he appears in life; in fact,

men as they are today are after all not such that one could love them with a healthy imagination. But in a woman's love there is always something more: there is an image which is the gift from that other world of the heavens. The man, on the other hand, loves with longing; the love of man carries an explicit character of wish. And this distinction must be made for it comes to expression both in the realm of ideas and of reality.

The woman sets out in love with her fantasy, and always forms an image of the one she loves—which is of course filled with fantasy. Man's love on the other hand is connected with wishes; his love bears the imprint of desires.

Again, here you have indications which are of the greatest importance for your subtle inner development, and for your understanding of what happens around you.

And now we will turn to this picture *(reproduced on page 34)*. Of course any anthroposophist looking at it will say: 'Quite clear; Lucifer and Ahriman'. But lo and behold Rudolf Steiner by no means called it 'Lucifer and Ahriman'. He called it 'Light and Shadow'. But it is much more. It is the polarity in the whole world which immediately arises when astrality starts to work. The light longs for the darkness; the male longs for the female; the acid longs for the base. This is expressed in the picture. The heat longs for the cold; the cold longs for the heat. The more you contemplate the picture, the more you will find that in fact in each one of our villagers, even in us, either this part of the image is more pronounced, or the other. *(Dr. König points to the upper red and lower blue sector of the picture.)* If you undertook a statistical survey, you would definitely discover that more women are like this *(red)* and more men are like that *(blue)*. If you look into each others' faces and compare your good ladies and yourself with this image you will soon find that here where the light is and there where the shadow is, two kinds of inner existence meet us in the following way.

Now we will try to describe and interpret this picture in spiritual terms. I will draw it.

Illustration 4

If you see one side like this, and the other side like that, then in between is the threshold. It is a threshold because from above our astral body looks with increasing intensity into the eyes, the nose, the tip of the nose, the lips, and you can see how exactly this is drawn. The intensity of the colour here increases towards the points, while below the intensity of the colours increases towards the frame, because this is the true image of the nervous system, to which the astrality looks down. Can you understand?

Here is the shadow of our brain, of our whole nervous system (all of which is actually nerve-substance); and our soul, in so far as it is astrality, looks towards this nerve-substance. Some of our handicapped friends are determined predominantly by their astrality, and what they do reflects in repetition, and how they act is imprint, is shadow, is going to become a shell with little content.

Others—many in the main part of their existence—are beyond the threshold, and they speak and act in a way that appears strange, un-understandable, erratic, stupid, because there is an existence beyond the threshold which we must recognise and more and more learn to understand; an existence in the sphere of light which is the astrality. And somehow the body acts erratically because from beyond the threshold what is here in the shadow part of the picture cannot be reached. In the ordinary person these two realms are better integrated. But you well know how difficult it is in the morning sometimes, with the most wonderful ideas and images, to make them real and bring them back into life.

So we have a morning existence and we have, let us say, an evening existence. We have to understand a light existence and a shadow existence. But the shadow existence is to a great extent, although not completely, identical with our nerves, whereas the light existence is identical with our astrality. And now when you walk around among our friends, you will immediately recognise, not in the build, not in the form, but for instance in their behaviour or in the colour of their skin, whether they live more in the light realm or more in the shadow realm. Don't mix this up with intellectuality and will—that would be quite wrong. The whole thing is astrality and nervous system. You might also say it is fantasy, imaginative life, flaming fire of images, and the shadow and the ash of our nervous system—which of course can also act as if something stood behind it, because the nervous system has the ability to repeat what was once upon a time put into it.

To distinguish between these two is another step in learning more and more to order the phenomena which you meet in your immediate surroundings. So if you start, for instance, not merely to look at this picture and say it is 'Lucifer and Ahriman', but to paint it, to draw it, to ponder about it, then you will develop something within you which is of the greatest help in your work.

We did not learn many facts today, but we could acquire some points of view. Thank you.

Discussions with Dr. König

Comment. Throughout yesterday and today, the mask has become more and more understandable to us and also our concepts have become wider.

You described the mask as being closely connected with the sentient soul—and we could see the first breaking through of the individuality with the dawn of the consciousness soul. There are so many characters walking about!

Dr. König. They used to walk about once. The more light you see, the more shadow is also there, so to speak. In some villages even today you find real characters. In the village life of former times each individuality took on a mask, and the village was complete when the masquerade was a complete one. You had a number of shepherds, ploughmen, blacksmiths, some misers, some wealthy people, a burgomaster, and all that. It was the education of the ego which had to go through one mask in one life, through another mask in another life, and thereby gradually more and more it achieved maturity.

Question. When looking at the original, unaltered life processes (Breathing, Warming, Nourishing and so on) this seems to me like a harmony in which the colouring of the character does not arise as yet. Where we have the influencing of these life processes through the Fall—so that they change into Consuming, Burning, Depositing, Sclerotising and so on—there arises something which already points strongly in the direction of character-formation. I was reminded of this again today when seeing the picture of Light and Shadow. There we have something like the colours of a rainbow—the two sides represented in the two corners where the faces appear. Each of them is formed into an archetypal character. Is it perhaps that the life processes can act as a kind of background, as a kind of fundamental colouring, to a first simple division of characters through the fact that they have—by Lucerific and Ahrimanic influence—been torn asunder in the way you described?

This gives rise as it were to a broad division in two—but of course when we look at characters, we have a practically infinite number of types. If one goes far enough, there seems to be no end. Why is this?

Dr. König. It is very interesting and already points in the direction I hope to take—not this year but next. We have our diagnostic key for the children, and in this diagnostic key we have twelve different types, which are, so to speak, the twelve consonants of form and *Gestalt* streaming down from the zodiac. Behind these there are also twelve masks which in each person, together with the seven-foldness of the life processes which have gone through the Fall, form out certain different types of masks. Now don't start to say seven times twelve is eighty-four, and therefore we have eighty-four masks. It would not work out like that, because there are probably a few masks which are outstanding, others which are very rare, and others which do not occur at all. But it is my impression that we can start to think in this way.

Question. If the astral is beyond the threshold and on earth in our physical existence there is something in which the astrality does not incarnate: are these two things together a mask, or is the mask this more or less empty bowl?

Dr. König. The bowl is the mask. It can be filled by the red (pointing to the picture). The chasm is always there, but there are bridges which can be trodden. The bridges can be destroyed however, and then there is no possibility of crossing. It is Goethe's fairy tale.

Comment. In the course of the last years, we have worked more and more with the curative diagnostic clock, and have found—especially when engaging in a closer study of the life process—that the realm of child hysteria and epilepsy were two fundamental aspects which we had not so much to consider, but rather to observe and deal with. Looking at this, I saw it as a wonderful illumination of something which we meet from the pastoral-medical point of view. What you described as the imaginative realm becoming sometimes too fiery was the one side and I would by no means wish to identify this with hysteria—only I feel that although it is different it is perhaps an equivalent to one of these two states or powers which we meet in epilepsy and hysteria in young children. It is a wonderful key which we have got, because the opposite can also happen, i.e. that the threshold is broken through too violently, and perhaps fifty or a hundred masks appear at the same time: astrality, world-astrality, simply pours into a mask existence that cannot sustain it and cannot change quickly enough.

Dr. König. I am particularly thankful that you say you are not going to relate it to hysteria or epilepsy, because one would immediately cut it short and pin it down to something which it is not. Sometimes it can appear like epilepsy or hysteria, but it is not. We should leave it fluid—as a guide and not a schemata. Therefore it is also not Lucifer and Ahriman.

Question. I want to ask if we would ever be called upon to deal with somebody in whom the nervous part is cut off entirely from the astrality. Would such a case come up where we could help?

Dr. König. You might be able to deal with a few, but only if the astrality appears and nakedly faces you. If there is only an empty shell and the bridges have disappeared you cannot do it. It will be invaded by other astrality, and you are powerless. . . I think some such cases are presented to us.

Comment. I sometimes have the feeling that what you described in the beginning, namely that the villagers are so unperturbed by all kinds of vicissitudes or happenings in life, while we always react very strongly, that this is due not only to masks, but also because they have built into themselves this chasm, this river, in a different way from us. Something heavenly lets them exist, while we exist to a great extent out of the customs of our mask. We don't react out of our higher existence to the vicissitudes of our life, but out of the mask.

Question. In the course of mankind's development the animals have remained behind and formed masks. . . is the form of a tree also a mask?

Dr. König. If you take 'the mask' in a very wide sense, you can say so—because in a sense the tree has a group-soul, and the *Gestalt* which this group-soul fashions could be called a mask.

Comment. Certain trees only reach their true form after fourteen years.

Dr. König. An apple tree would only become an apple tree in its form after fourteen years?

Comment. Yes—certain kinds of apple tree.

Dr. König. How amazing—that is a wonderful statement.

Question. I am reminded of the artist, whom we sometimes confront with great questions. How is an artist able to face such distortions, for instance, of a human countenance? Modern painters must be very open to perceiving the great varieties of the mask. Again and again we are faced with the question: Is this still art or beauty?

Dr. König. It is the mask formation in the astral world which they bring over—usually in a supersensible way. If you read the diaries of Paul Klee—you will see that he perceives out of his clairvoyance and what he perceives he paints.

Question. Where would one meet the manifestation or 'shining-through' of the ego? We have found that if we manage to make our young people work, very steadily and very properly, then they may not express their individuality in their work because that seems to be the mask—but nevertheless in doing so their individuality has much more chance to shine through at other moments. And when we listened to what was said yesterday, the appearance of the ego, of the individuality, seems to be a fleeting one. I wonder whether one could imagine that on this river a boat appears now and then—in which the individuality appears, even acting as a kind of temporary bridge between the two realms—and then disappears again?

Dr. König. The river is the individuality. This is the ego *(pointing to the green section of the picture)*. Therefore we do not recognise it in us. Can you understand?

Comment. When one looks at the mask as you described it—having in mind such novels as Dickens was able to write, where every character is so sharply defined—one has the impression that one is confronted by individuality. This quite obviously is a mistaken concept. On the other hand one would expect that in the age of the consciousness soul one would see the individuality emerging—yet no age has been so overburdened with 'average-ness'; where individuality is so much submerged.

Dr. König. Take a man like Gladstone—an amazing figure of the nineteenth century. He was a hero outwardly; a weak nobody inwardly: a little baby in his private life—a child in need of special care—yet of tremendous, imposing power when he stood up in the House of Commons. Hardly anyone dared to move. But you could flick your fingers and he would have fallen down—if you had done it out of the ego. The same, exactly the same applies to Bismarck. Here he was, the builder of the German Empire—and if you were to lift his jacket you would find a nice little person underneath who was told by his wife, "Go to bed, darling; it's late." And he would say, "Yes Mummy." The "Yes, Mummy" is an expression of the ego—but the astrality is carrying all destiny. . . If I remember I will quote you some lines from a lecture of Rudolf Steiner, in which he describes the astral body as the carrier of our past destiny. This becomes manifest when we go over the threshold. Astrality as it were disperses. It is a process of exhaling and widening, and then it comes together again in a kind of inhaling. Then we take it with us and in our next incarnation appear in the right guise. This is not personality. Hamlet was a personality, because he was so flabbergasted by his own existence. Many other things—thinking, feeling and willing, for instance, play into this: only to begin with we should be careful not to mix things up. Astrality is full of egoism. All these men are egoists—but it is not *the* ego which is in control. . . . The true ego is always altruistic.

Comment. This is very interesting and very important. The last century is remarkable by reason of the great figures of Church and State. They were giants, but where are they today? There were surely exceptions. I think Abraham Lincoln was an exception; he was different from Gladstone and Disraeli. There were others too.

Dr. König. Where would you think the difference is?

Comment. With Lincoln the true ego shone through, but I cannot say why and how.

Dr. König. It would be wrong, dear friends, if you were to think that where the ego appears everything is weak. Yet the ego is a baby. The figure of Christophorus is a wonderful image of what we are now talking about. The giant carrying the child, and breaking down under the power of this tiny little thing—in the river, of course.

Comment. The river has a great deal to do with it. There were certain figures who had a special mission in the preparation of the Michael Age.

Dr. König. I am convinced of that.

Comment. I feel that the imagination which Dr. König put before us in the morning will unfold its great power of help for us—particularly when we try to use it as a means to understand not only the handicapped person, but also ourselves—because it holds good also for ourselves. I think of the strange change that one can observe in modern literature—when the ego awakens and the consciousness soul begins, and men describe themselves as undifferentiated, very nearly identical. We are tempted to think that we are different from each other by virtue of our different egos. Inasmuch as we experience our astrality, it contains all that has already been experienced. If we were to really meet our ego—if we would have to pick it out of a big heap—I don't know how we would find it. That is a very important realisation in our meeting with the young people. We are inclined to believe that it is the nature of our ego whereby we can guide them. It is not. Rather it is the position which the point occupies in the magnitude of events. If we learn to use this image that our ego works as a torch beam or as a point we will gain a quite different possibility to meet the problem. Our astrality is the great power and force, and we have all the time to cope with it ourselves. . . .

Comment. I don't think we are sufficiently strong to influence the young people with our ego. We can help them in two directions. On the one hand we have to educate and control our own astral impulses, and on the other we can, if we have the will, direct something towards the being of our young people which can work through them, but it is not of the ego nature. If we have the will, we can hand to them the gift of all our awareness and concern, which enables one to deal with a whole lot of problems. In return they do something for us. They have an innate acceptance of life, which we are not even beginning to approach. And out of this, in the background of their existence, they give us enormous strength.

Dr. König. They still experience themselves immediately in the hands of God because they are not yet fully at one with their physical-earthly existence as we have to be; and this is their faith. I would still like to add something to what has just been said. If you read, for instance, some of the outstanding novels of the twentieth century, where the nature of the ego is described, you will find that one of them was written in Paris and another in Vienna. There is the book by Marcel Proust, *Rememberance of Things Past*.[4] Then there is Rilke. They suddenly begin to observe this little ego.

Question. During yesterday afternoon's discussion about the nest and the home—the word 'brotherliness' suddenly entered into our concern. Thomas described that the egos are difficult to distinguish— and what makes us distinguishable is much rather the nature of our astrality. I wonder whether it is not the nature of our astrality together with the fact that our growing egos are not the same, that is the basis of what appears as brotherliness? I thought of this image of Christophorus in connection with what our task really is. I was a bit doubtful yesterday whether the old kind of family can be the basis of our village work. Will we not have to find a different concept for the future family? Is not the meeting in warmth, the meeting of the brothers in Christ, the whole basis of our work in the villages?

Comment. Some weeks ago you proposed to Newton Dee to turn much more to the musical element. I must connect this with what you said on music three years ago when you stressed the importance of the interval, where one ego can most intimately meet the other.

Dr. König. It is in our training centres where this is so important.

Question. Towards the end of your lecture you made a remark which I could not quite follow—in connection with the nerve substance being able to retain what has been put into it.

Dr. König. We are born more or less with a brain and a spine which is an empty blank tablet. Our experiences—on the one hand by means of our senses, on the other hand by means of our motor-activities— are gradually inscribed into certain districts and parts of this tablet. The more this is done, the better we acquire habits. If we learn to write or to drive a car, or to ride a bike, it also depends on the way in which it is inscribed into these tablets of our nervous substance. They have the possibility to act independently. A fit, for instance—an involuntary movement—all such things give the possibility of repetition without our consciousness being present. This is what I meant.

Third Lecture

Karl König

Given on the morning of 12th January 1962

Dear Friends,

This morning we will try to take a further step towards developing a first insight into the knowledge of the mask, which has gradually started to reveal itself in its astral existence. This has become the keynote of our meeting. Now it is a fact that Rudolf Steiner, after thirty years of pondering, meditating and gaining clarifying insight, has handed over to the twentieth century an entirely new image of man. He described man as a threefold being, not only as to his physical body but also in the realm of the soul, and in the realm of the spirit. We too, must gradually find the connections, the bridges, the interweaving structures between these three spheres of existence. In the education of the child and the young person this threefold image does not play as direct and immediate a part as one would expect. In our work with handicapped children, for instance, we are not immediately concerned—and I emphasise 'immediately'—we are not immediately concerned with the threefold being of man. It is always difficult to try to assess a handicapped or an ordinary child according to the threefold structure of his or her existence, because in childhood and youth this threefold image of man is not yet an open, a revealed secret. Only after man has fully matured, only after we have passed our twentieth year, does the threefold being of our existence come into its own. If we study children, either ordinary or handicapped, or if we study the traits, conditions and constitutions of teenagers, there stands in the background like a huge, archetypal image, the threefold being of man. It stands in the background influencing indirectly, as it were, all our ideas and concepts: about childhood and single children, about youth and single people.

Therefore we have to find other means to understand them. Over the years we had to develop, for instance, the twelvefold diagnostic key which proved very helpful with our handicapped children. In a similar way, we spoke yesterday about the picture 'Light and Shadow', this image of light and darkness. We tried to approach it as a meditative key for an understanding of our teenagers. We will gradually have to learn that here, as it were, the situation of man during and after puberty is revealed. It would be too coarse to say 'this is man between the fourteenth and twenty-first year'; it would be quite wrong to make such a statement. But if we say 'after puberty', then it can also mean on into the fifties and sixties, because there are many who do not grow beyond puberty, even if they are thirty or forty. You know this.

But something else gradually begins to play into this when human beings mature physically and mentally. The maturing process starts to heal what is brought about by the split into male and female. After puberty, this healing process leads from the twofold, polar existence of the teenager to the gradually unfolding threefoldness of man. The new trinity presents itself in many ways and in multiple possibilities as the human being gradually develops his threefold existence. The threefoldness of existence has to more and more become the meditative key for those who live responsibly in our villages. In the training centres it is a twofoldness: in the villages it is a threefoldness. And it is just in this threefoldness, precisely in the way in which Rudolf Steiner indicated—he did no more than indicate—that you find what will gradually give you the measure for all the masks which appear.

You remember that I said we will have to learn the values of the different masks. We cannot compare one mask with the other; we must learn to measure it, not in a mathematical sense but in the sense of value. And the value of the mask lies entirely in its relation to the threefoldness of man. There is a chapter in Rudolf Steiner's book *Von Seelenrätseln* (*Riddles of the Soul*), where the key is given to the threefold being of man. The chapter is entitled *Die physischen und geistigen Abhängigkeiten* (*Interdependence of the physical and spiritual aspects of the human being)*. As far as I am aware this book, which is one of the fundamental books by Rudolf Steiner, has never been translated into English.[5] Not only is the physical and mental threefoldness described in this chapter, but also what is so especially important for you, namely the description of the threefold physique in relation to Imagination, Inspiration, and Intuition: for instance in a sentence like this . . .

> *Und wie der Leib in seinem Bereich nach zwei Seiten das Wesen seiner Aussenwelt miterleben lässt, nämlich in den Sinnes und den Bewegungsvorgängen, so der Geist nach der einen Seite hin, indem er das vorstellende Seelenleben auch im gewöhnlichen Bewusstsein* imaginativ *erlebt; und nach der andern Seite hin, indem er im Wollen* intuitive *Impulse ausgestaltet, die sich durch Stoffwechselvorgänge verwirklichen.*

Permit me an aside before translating this—and please don't take it amiss! I say this with reference to those who work in the villages. If those who wish to be responsible village workers do not educate their own thinking abilities, then the thinking will be as muddled (and has already started to become so) as at times the life in the village households is. Anthroposophia will have to be your guide in everything you do. Understanding of the threefold being of man will only be gained if clearly ordered thinking illuminates at least a few of you. I do not mean intellect; I mean the clear thinking exemplified in the above sentences. Rudolf Steiner says:

> And as the body is connected in its realm in a twofold way with the surrounding world, in as far as it manifests sensory activity as well as motor activity, in the same way the spirit is connected with the twofold activity of Imagination and Intuition.*

I will only indicate this. I leave it to you to study it further. These are

---

* And as the body, in its domain, allows the existence of the external world to be experienced in two directions, namely in the sense processes and in movement activity, so does the spirit experience on the one hand the conceptualising life of the soul *imaginatively* even in ordinary consciousness, and on the other hand forms *intuitive* impulses in the will which are realised through metabolic processes. *Editor's translation.*

contents for your College Meeting.

Or take a sentence like this from the same chapter:

> *So wie im Leibe durch das rhythmische Geschehen sich der*
> *sterbliche Teil des fühlenden Menschenwesens offenbart, so*
> *in dem Inspirations-Inhalt des schauenden Bewusstseins*
> *der unsterbliche geistige Seelenwesenskern.*

> Just as the finite or mortal part of the feeling being of man is
> revealed in the physical body through rhythmical processes,
> so is the immortal spiritual kernel of the soul being
> revealed in the inspirational content of its visionary
> consciousness.

This, dear friends, is principally for your guidance. Please don't
think that because you have heard so much about the threefold
being of man, about the sensory-nerve being, about the rhythmical
being, and the metabolic-limb being, that you have more than a few
hazy concepts. Of course you know that there is thinking, there is
feeling and there is willing, and that it works. Of course it works:
indeed it works very well. However, we must not only understand it;
we must also gradually learn to use it as a key in applying the image
of the threefold being of man to the whole world. Dear friends, only
this—and again I say something which I feel is of great importance,
and so I repeat the words which Rudolf Steiner used time and
again—only this will make it possible for a true threefold social
order to become established where you work. For the threefold
order in the social realm is not something which can be
superimposed on any social organism; it has to grow from within. It
is the result of the effort of the single human being to learn to live
with an understanding of the threefold being of man. The more you
concern yourself with the concept of threefoldness, not in the social
realm but in the being of man, the more directly, immediately, the
social structure will turn into a threefold existence, because you
order it from within. You order it from within, magically. Magically,
dear friends, it will emerge, whether you like it or not, and suddenly
you will see: it is the threefold social order. So it is.

And now let us go a step further. Let us try to develop the first mask out of an understanding of the threefold being of man. It is going to be a little bit easier now. Shortly after the beginning of the age of the consciousness soul—not immediately, but two or three centuries later—there was an awakening of the ego in man, characterised in a special way. Attempts were made not only to classify the animal kingdom, or the mineral kingdom, but also to classify man. And the classification of men, into races, types and so on, is an undertaking which was first accomplished by occultists. John Battista Porta,[6] for instance, and others like him, tried to discover the differences between the various peoples. They asked themselves: Are there only individuals or can we see, among the individuals, certain general traits? You know that Lavater[7] tried to discover—and the whole science of physiognomy is related to this one great question—whether the human kingdom is at all divisible in a general way and not only in individual terms. Is it similar, for instance, to dogs, which can be distinguished by very many different forms? Imagine a bulldog, a dachshund, a spaniel or whatever; how different they are. And yet they are all dogs: no one knows why. But yet the differences in man, for example his build, are not as large or astonishing as they are in dogs. Certainly we have started to distinguish the various races, for instance, yet it has been found that there are other dividing lines which cut right across the races— which one finds among the white man as well as the yellow and the black—and some very important steps have been made, although not until this century.

The first important and very revealing discovery (although something of it was known before, but it now came as a scientific discovery) was made by the German psychiatrist Kretschmer[8] when he suddenly began to describe how the physical build and temperamental structure of a man can coincide; and I say 'can coincide', I don't say 'must coincide'. For instance, he described two basic physical builds, the pyknic type and the leptosom (asthenic) type of man: the pyknic type being like this – ( ) – and the leptosom like this –| |. To this he added the cyclotymic and the schizotymic temperaments. I will say a few words about this in a moment. From his long experience as a psychiatrist he was able to discover that a great number of schizophrenic people have a different bodily structure than those suffering from another type of mental illness, the manic-depressive condition, in which there is a kind of rhythmic disorder between melancholia and mania. He found that generally the pyknic type of person tends more towards the manic-depressive condition, whereas about ninety per cent of schizophrenics are of the leptosom type.* Dear friends, it is a very fundamental discovery—if you don't take it as an absolute, if you don't think: Here is an elongated man, so naturally he must be schizoid, or in the end become a schizophrenic, but if instead you say the following: This person (if he is a leptosom, meaning if he is elongated and thinnish) tends to have a more or less melancholic temperament. The melancholic temperament is generally connected with a physical structure in which the nerve processes are stronger than all the others, or in which the other processes are so weak that the nerve processes overpower the whole life of such a person. On the other hand you find that the pyknic person is built in such a way that his metabolic process is stronger than the rhythmic and the head-nerve processes. If you follow this direction you will gradually discover that, of course, everyone tends in some way or another either towards the pyknic, or towards the leptosom type; that is, he has schizoid traits, or manic-depressive traits. Can you understand what I mean? This is no pigeon-holing in which the short, thick ones are placed here and the long, thin ones are contained in another pigeon-hole there, but that there is always the potential, in more or less both directions, at least to a certain extent. The most interesting thing is that Kretschmer never classified women; he only classified men. I don't know why. He was obviously a gentleman. I have never asked him, but it would be interesting to find out why he did so. I am certain that he did so because women cannot be classified in the same way as men.**

Now a much greater step forward was made exactly one moon-node period (eighteen years and seven months) after Kretschmer's discovery, and it was made in the West. It was achieved after many,

---

*   Figures refer to patients in his mental hospital.

** A statement by Rudolf Steiner given in 1916 that is relevant to this discussion is to be found in Appendix B.

many years of painstaking work on several thousand men at Harvard University in the U.S.A. by a man called Sheldon. He discovered something which he considered to be entirely new, although it was in fact a better, truer, more direct, more intimate confirmation of the as yet hazy ideas of the German Kretschmer. Sheldon has written many books. The most revealing one concerning his work is called *The Varieties of Temperament*,[9] in which he describes three physical structures, bodily structures: the endomorph, the mesomorph and the ectomorph. To the doctors I would like to say, endoderm, mesoderm, ectoderm. He describes their physical structure somewhat like this. I shall make three drawings.

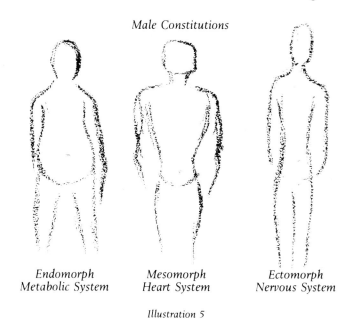

Male Constitutions

| *Endomorph* | *Mesomorph* | *Ectomorph* |
| *Metabolic System* | *Heart System* | *Nervous System* |

Illustration 5

1) The endomorph: a roundish head, not too elongated neck, somewhat drooping shoulders, and thin, usually rather short arms; a rather short chest and a good tummy—very good—in the centre of which is the navel; and then quite well-filled upper thighs; thin lower legs and feet.

2) The mesomorph: usually taller than the endomorph and with a square head and a strong neck; broad shoulders (I am exaggerating a bit, to make myself understood); mighty arms, and a square chest. They are present among us, although not in such exaggeration. And it is very interesting that the loins are tapering. They are perfect runners. I describe only men, dear friends.

3) The ectomorph: a person who is also rather tall. In Vienna we say an *Eierkopf* (egg-head). A long neck; very long, hanging shoulders; the chest, as you can imagine, long and lean; there is never enough room considering the length. This is the ectomorph.

You can already see now what it is about. You find very typically here (1) *(pointing to Illustration 5)* that the metabolic process is prominent; here (2) the motor and circulatory process is in the foreground; while here (3) there is predominantly nervous activity. You will find, just in our villagers, dear friends, how these three types are much more pronounced, much more clear-cut, much more mask-like than in any ordinary person. Here (1) the navel, the umbilicus so to speak, is the centre of existence. Here (2) the centre of existence is the muscle of the heart: not what we call the heart, but the muscle of the heart. The centre of this existence (3) is in the forebrain. Don't think of females please, we will come to them later.

Sheldon's great step forward is the following. He described not only the physical structure, but also the temperament pertaining to that structure, although not in our sense of the temperaments which Rudolf Steiner described as the four temperaments in connection with the Hippocratic teaching. Sheldon describes the temperaments, the mental traits, of these three types as a kind of reactive behaviour, which is no doubt exceedingly typical for each of these three. Naturally, a man like Sheldon does not think of the higher being of man. He is under the impression that what he has described simply makes these three types of people what they are. It is dreadful sometimes to read with what disdain he speaks about this poor creature Man, who has no choice other than to behave according to his physique. I point this out so that you can see I do recognise the good sides of Sheldon, but I also know his limitations—and he has tremendous limitations. But he has described the three types in such a way that he also gives them new names; names which I feel are absolutely right. He calls the traits of the endomorph, viscerotonia (viscerum is the intestine); those of the mesomorph he calls somatotonia (from soma—body) and those of the ectomorph, cerebrotonia (from 'cerebrum'—brain).* (1) Viscerotonia, (2) Somatotonia, (3) Cerebrotonia; you can accept this nomenclature, or leave it, as you wish. But you see that this largely coincides with the threefold human being as we describe him.

Now what are some of the main traits? From his statistics Sheldon has worked out sixty different traits; twenty for each of the three physical constitutions. I will describe these first of all, giving you more indications. I will describe them so that you have an idea of the way in which this man is trying to understand them. For instance, he says of viscerotonia that the main trait is relaxation, general relaxation. He is a man who loves comfort; who loves to sit, not on a hard chair, but on an easy chair. He is a man who has the trait of being sociable, sometimes without any discrimination; of being friendly to everybody. Food plays a rather important part in his daily life: he likes to eat. He likes to eat a well-cooked meal, and with company, and he likes to enjoy the time after the meal, the digestive process. All this causes him to structure his surroundings as comfortably as possible. He likes to be surrounded by nice things. He needs to be approved by others. He also very often needs to lean on others, to be comforted by others. And he is definitely against any form of physical exercise such as climbing, marching, skiing, skating, so that he tries to avoid any kind of sport entirely. These, to begin with, are some of the traits of viscerotonia.

The man with somatotonia has entirely different traits. His dominant trait is *motor* activity. He comes into a room and simply cannot sit still. He will go and shake hands with everyone; his approach to everyone will be utterly direct: he will tell them what he is and why he is; what he thinks and what he does. Every kind of activity is an absolute necessity for him. After a ten hour walk he will come in and start to box, for instance. Then quite suddenly he will

---

* See Appendix C for Sheldon's Table of Traits.

be tired, have a few hours sleep and in the morning rise early. This is the kind of man, for instance, who looks for danger; who wants to get into dangerous situations. He wants to do something where danger is lurking ahead of him. But the one thing he will never be able to understand is loneliness. These are people who suffer from a high degree of claustrophobia, which means they cannot stand being shut in a room by themselves; at least the windows and doors must be open. If he and another of his type enter a room of thirty or forty people, it will be just these two who make all the necessary—and unnecessary—noise. They will always speak out quite loudly. You can imagine how they behave if you have ever observed some Dutch people. You cannot possibly miss the trait if you observe two or three Dutch people together. Loudness itself. Unconcern. Nobody else in the world exists: that is somatotonia. Now don't take this as an absolute because we all have this trait to some extent; even if we are endomorphs, we are at times somatotonic.

Cerebrotonia is entirely different. The main trait, dear friends, is restraint, inhibition, particularly in the social realm. Such persons have the greatest difficulty to say a loud word, or to speak in a melodious way. They will start a sentence, then say "Oh dear, I can't express myself." If, for instance, you observe them sitting, you will notice that they will not only fold one leg over the other but make a double fold, and they always hold their hands behind them, or in their pockets. These are people who, when they come to talk to you, will never take off their coat. They will perhaps take off their hat and then they will sit down, but only just; only on the edge of the chair. "What I want to say . . . perhaps you could tell me what you think." This, dear friends, is something we have to learn to understand. It is not simply funny, it is often exceedingly uncomfortable for those who suffer from it and those who have to suffer with it. For such a person who is, as it were, destined by the cerebrum, by his brain, is as enclosed in his world as his brain is enshrined in the skull.

The reactions of these people to certain events in the world around them are very different. I will give you one example and leave it to you to find others. How would each of the three types react if, for instance, a close relative whom he loved dearly suddenly dies? The endomorph would try to gather around him as many people as possible, in order to be comforted and to say, 'You see what I have suffered and how terrible it is for me now that I am lonely'. He is surrounded by six, eight or ten acquaintances and friends because he can only console himself when he is with others. What will the mesomorph do? He might, for instance, take an axe and fell a tree, or get into his car and go on a five hundred mile drive, or he might decide that he must climb a mountain. He cannot just go to the funeral, he has to express himself in his mobility and movement. He has no other form of expression. And the ectomorph will turn the key of his room and stay put, quite lonely. He does not want to see anybody; does not want to be disturbed by anybody: nothing! You see, you must learn to understand that some of your young men will, after they feel they have been insulted for instance, suddenly go and do something to work it off. I could of course go on describing these traits to a much greater extent. (See Appendix for Sheldon's table of traits.) I have put these three types before you in order to show you how the threefold man begins to reveal himself in physical constitution and mental traits, especially in people where the metabolic system, the rhythmic system and the cerebral or nervous system is overdeveloped.

However, the question has to be asked: How does this apply to women? I have not investigated it as thoroughly as Sheldon, but I have tried to make my own observations throughout the last fifteen or twenty years. I believe that three very typical and relevant types can also be found in women. I will again try to draw them. *(see page 66)*

And now let us look at the following. When Rudolf Steiner spoke about threefold man he clearly formulated *metabolic-limb* system, and he clearly formulated *sensory-nerve* system. Can you see what I am getting at? This, the metabolic system, is the male, and this, the limb system, is the female. The nervous system is the male, the sensory system is the female. Because the nerve/sensory system is male/female; the metabolic/limb system is male/female. The rhythmic system, the heart/lung system, is also male/female. So we have only to find the respective female type of the metabolic system: it is the limb female. Now I am not thinking of anyone in particular; rather it is just from experiences which I have had over the years that I might also call this type microcephalic. Quite a good, extended

Female Constitutions

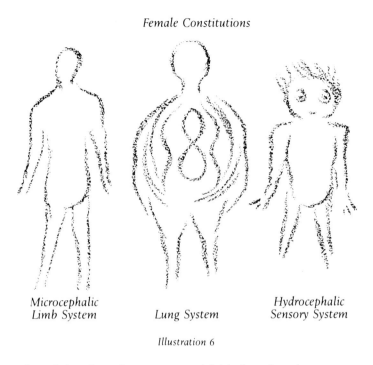

Microcephalic
Limb System

Lung System

Hydrocephalic
Sensory System

Illustration 6

neck and then long, long arms, and fairly long legs (women never have very long legs, but fairly long legs). I am trying first to describe the physical structure. They are fairly powerfully muscular; they represent the limb system over against the metabolic system represented by men.

Then a second type, and I will now take the sensory type before I go on to the middle group. If we could call the limb type microcephalic, then the sensory type is hydrocephalic—a comparatively large head, very tender limbs, and a very tender, sometimes infantile, bodily structure. I hope I am not being too outspoken. They have large eyes, beautiful eyes, and a huge forehead, lovely hair and a tiny nose. They are somewhat hypersensitive, talking too much, are interested in very many different things and always a little bit active. This is the match to the cerebrotonic.

Then comes the last type, the middle group. The rhythmical

system is the dominant feature taking in even the lower parts of the trunk, and the older they grow the more they take everything in. The head is fairly round. You understand that I have drawn this with a certain amount of hesitation, but it is like this. The traits are not so easily described. You will find, for instance in our young villagers, many of the rhythmic type (2), many of the limb type (1), and a few of the sensory type (3). The hypersensory type—we could well call it this—the hypersensory type is the lonely type. They find it difficult to make contact; they prefer to be on their own. They tend much more to the company of women than to the company of men. They have fleeting connections with men; they will attract a man and then repulse him again very quickly, because they want but can't. They attract, and yet they are so sensitive that any nearness of the other sex makes them uneasy and is unwarranted: they like it and at the same time dislike it. It is also not easy for them to do any kind of housework. The rhythmic type are the perfect housewives, the perfect workers. They can do with any kind of man. They are the ones who rule the house; they are easy going but can be quite outspoken at times. They rule the workshop and do things with a certain amount of lust and gusto. The limb type are those who serve and never tire of serving. They do and continue doing. They are the ones who are immensely faithful; they are faithful even in their unfaithfulness. There is a certain amount of continuity in them on which one can build, yet they can be erratic in their behaviour. They will suddenly say 'no' and then they will leave a house, a man, their work, and do something entirely different. In a situation such as an accident they will be the only ones who are level-headed. The sensory type will run away in terror, trying to protect themselves, the rhythmic type will at first be somewhat upset, overcome themselves within a few minutes, and then be the perfect mothers. The rhythmic type is the mother; the sensory type is the sister; the limb type is the companion.

Go gradually further, try to see these three types and connect them in the way in which I have tried to describe them. Here (1) *(pointing to Illustration 6)* it is the limbs; here (2) it is the lung, not the heart; here (3) it is the senses: they have big ears; they hear everything, see everything, and so on.

Dear friends, in this way the idea of the threefoldness in male and female will have to be developed, so that these six masks will help you to understand the reactive behaviour, the mental attitudes, of those with whom you live. But again I warn you not to be too direct in connecting the masks to the living images which you meet. Try to build it up within yourselves, and learn to say to yourselves that here (3) *(pointing again to Illustration 6)* they live much more towards Imagination in the true sense of the word, here (2) toward Inspiration and here (1) toward Intuition. You will soon discover that you can rely on the intuition of those who have some of the traits referred to in the microcephalic female. You can rely on what they say, because through their voice something much wiser than they themselves are reveals itself. They are the type for instance, who in former times were the ones who uttered what the gods wanted to speak to man. And you can rely on the fantasy, wonder and beauty which the hydrocephalic types produce out of a higher imagination. If you then try to lift it up within yourselves, to lift it one step higher than where we ourselves are, you will engender in those around you the impulse to recognize themselves. And if then, pondering about it again, you see it in its connection with the threefoldness, in female and in male, then more and more something will develop which will really anchor the outer life of the villagers to the rock of knowledge of the threefold being of man. This is what I wanted to say.

Discussions with Dr. König

Comment. I had to link your words this morning with what you spoke about yesterday, particularly the novels you advised us to read, and of course I thought especially of Charles Dickens. As you drew the three types of men I saw three characters. The first one was Micawber, who was always waiting for something to turn up—and who was so often annoyed with David though he loved him very much. And then in the centre I saw Bill Sykes, who was always looking for danger, and for Little Nell. If you read how Dickens described them, what you spoke about is well illustrated in the novel. Then for the third one you have Uriah Heap. I am a little more diffident about the women. Yet here you have Little Nell (3). Now for the middle one you have the housekeeper in *David Copperfield*, who looked after David so well—Peggoty. And then of course you have the Aunt, who as soon as she saw David wanted to give him a bath (1).

Dr. König. Thank you very much. I don't need any more confirmation than that.

Question. May I turn to something entirely different. First of all I want to express my thanks for the very clear way in which this has been presented by Dr. König. There is however one thing which is not quite clear to me. The mesomorph or somatotonic type in the middle represents a mainly muscular type—it is the one in which you described the heart as being the centre of his existence. In a way he develops not only into his limbs, but into muscles and limbs. The female type on the left however, is also a muscular type. There seems to be a certain overlapping and yet something that does not quite coincide. Why is it that the heart type male (the mesomorph) in the middle and the limb type female on the left both go so much into the limb system—and yet in an entirely different way? What does the heart type have to do with the limb and motor development and what is the differentiating point between the two?

Dr. König. As far as I can see it, the mesomorphic male, (the somatotonic) is not so much a limb type, but rather a muscular type; this is his dominating feature. He can well be a small man. I had a colleague, for instance, who was hardly taller than I, yet he was a typical mesomorph. You know this is the type who looks at his watch like this (gesture, emphatic arm movement) or who would make this gesture before he sits down. I also said it is the heart muscle. It is not the limb. The mesomorph is hypertonic and also usually has a somewhat higher blood pressure. Of course the muscles are mainly connected with our limbs, therefore the limbs in this type are usually large.

Here, with the female type, the limbs are large because the head is so small; they are large because something is working down here instead of building up thoughts and ideas. This is a very clear differentiation. Sometimes you will find in these females also a certain mesomorphic trait, but never as clearly as in the mesomorphic male.

Comment. I think the question just raised is a very immediate one. I believe it has something to do with the fact that these types have been recorded—by Kretschmer as well as by Sheldon—as types, as exaggerations. In our age the hypertonic type, which is really the mesomorphic type, has been looked upon as if it were the norm and the others were the deviations. That is a complete misunderstanding. These are types which only appear at all through the incarnation— and if the incarnation becomes too one sided then these exaggerated types appear.

The norm is that the three are a balanced unity. The athletic type has been idealised. This type (the ectomorph) was called by our gym teacher 'the little runt'. He was a rather small man but a real phenomenon. He had a totally square head set on a triangle, and the triangle set on tiny legs. He could hold his arm horizontally for five minutes. The athletic type is a harmonious type only together with the other two. It is the blend of the three. The mesomorphic type is just as pathological and extreme as the endomorphic or the ectomorphic type.

Dr. König. How right this is comes out very clearly in Sheldon, because in the middle of his book he describes in three consecutive chapters the ideal but exaggerated three types; and at the end he poses the question: How are we going to heal each type? These three types are entirely deviant if they appear in an absolute way.

Question. Is it not the case that what appears in the mask in its manifold differentiations is much stronger than the individuality, at least for the moment? The ego in our time is like a baby; the Egyptian Gods with animal heads are more powerful. The individuality as such is higher, but the types are more powerful. They are powerful because the ego which is meant eventually to comprise them all is still a baby.

Dr. König. What we do is nothing else, dear friends, than to develop within us what in Egyptian culture was put before the people, namely the Sphinx. It is the Sphinx which we are talking about, and it is much more powerful than our ego. It has the power of the astral builders of the universe.

Comment. This is a very telling remark. The other day I saw a book about archaic Attic tombstones. And there in quite early times—between eight hundred and six hundred years before Christ—the Sphinx is carved on this gravestone, as if the individuality had gone into the lap of God and the mask is left on earth.

Question. Observing the three male types and the three female types one may wonder whether or not all six belong to the human being in his wholeness? It becomes more striking through your presentation than it usually is by ordinary observation.

Dr. König. In the male these *(pointing to the three female types)* are the three etheric bodies. In the female the other three are the etheric bodies.

Comment. I am so impressed when I see these three male types in connection with what Rudolf Steiner says about the different nations. The first one (the endomorph) has characteristics of the Italian, who needs a companion but remains a stranger. The second one is the German, (the mesomorph) who sees the enemy everywhere. The third one is the Englishman, who is the competitor, the rival.

Dr. König. Hardly anyone knows this lecture you are referring to. It is in Cycle XXXIX,[10] which Rudolf Steiner gave immediately after the outbreak of the First World War. I find this remark of the greatest importance. So this would already be a help for you in one of your Chapter Meetings; just to find sufficient openness for this, then to deal with the reactions.

Comment. The Italian is the stranger. And of course this little man (the endomorph) cannot bear it that there are any strangers. The German always sees the enemy; imagines the attack. The Englishman is the competitor, the rival whom he cannot tolerate.

Another thought occured to me as you were speaking. In the Curative Course Dr. Steiner says that one can only help children by, for instance, working with one's ego on their astrality, i.e, always on the next lower member. We must try to get so far that we can work with the ego. In the lecture he gave on prayer Dr. Steiner said that the greatest strengthening of the human ego is given through the possibility of prayer.

Question. These masks only emerge gradually at the time of puberty, especially between the fourteenth and the eighteenth year. Would we not have to try in our training centres to bring about some healing in a very special way, which later on can no longer be done?

Dr. König. Perhaps this is possible, but I wonder whether we can do it in the present state of our experience and knowledge.

Comment. I have the feeling it could not really be done; at least not in regard to making them better or more normal. I am sure a certain amount of 'curative education' should still be used in order to enlarge their world and their future. But I don't think one can heal them after their fourteenth year.

Dr. König. One can give them more masks to wear than the fundamental mask they have chosen.

Question. I would like to bring up a question which indirectly, I think, has a certain importance. I have been startled by the tolerance for each other that develops among the villagers, and which I feel exceeds our own capacities for tolerance. That we find difficulty with tolerance arises through our just not being a true manifestation of our own individuality. I imagine that the total incarnation would be completely tolerant. Why have the villagers fallen into such one-sidedness and yet have this exceptional capacity for tolerance? If we could learn to understand this we might be helped to find a degree of tolerance comparable to theirs.

Dr. König. I have the following impression. We ordinary people connect ourselves much more directly and intimately with our constitution, and therefore our constitution becomes part of our individual existence. The villagers wear their constitution like a mask, and therefore they carry it in front of them but they themselves remain behind, and this is the tolerance which they have. I think that this is one answer. When we spoke about it yesterday, I mentioned how amazing it is to observe how many different kinds of animals live together in the wild without any kind of enmity. You see birds and beasts of prey and elephants going around the same shore of the same lake, and they would never dream of attacking each other, whereas similar types of animals would not tolerate the invasion of their special territory—because they also wear their mask, but independently of their individuality, which we do not do. I could imagine it in this way.

Comment. It is perhaps important that we should not think that the essential help will flow from our studying the types in our villagers. To begin with we should try to find a greater distance between our own constitutional type and our own consciousness. I believe that what Dr. König has revealed could become a quite essential help in order to develop greater tolerance towards the villagers, inasmuch as we would learn to separate ourselves—to make a slight step back from our own mask—so that we would see our own mask as one of the many masks that live in the village. On a certain level we might thereby become one with the villagers, but also more free, and that would allow an increased tolerance.

Question. I wanted to say something on the problem of guiding young people in the training centres. In our fairly young endeavour at Glencraig* we have observed that all those we take into the training experience immediate relief at being free from schooling and curative education, at being granted the opportunity to work and to engage in all that is connected with it. This enables them to express themselves in one or the other mask. Should we try at this point to acquaint them (or give them) further masks or should we wait and observe? In the training centres do we still have the possibility of creating further masks which the young people can use in later life in the villages?

I felt that the training centres might have the task of continuing in one way what is begun in the schools where we try to foster self-expression in reading, writing and so forth. In the training centre we do this in a different way: through work. Here they establish themselves more, I feel. It is a tremendous grace that we have the training centres, though formal education must still continue. But, under the general heading of education, training sets in up to the eighteenth year.

Question. We build our own earthly temples; we are responsible. Therefore the type we are is not an accident. And with regard to our young people, would it be right for us, in the course of this study, perhaps to ask why he is this type, or she is that type?

---

* Glencraig Curative Schools, Northern Ireland, at that time a combined school and village. Editor.

Question. To refer to the former question, I wonder whether or not the whole realm of art should permeate the training?

Dr. König. There is no doubt: art and world experience. These are the two things which we must foster beside the work. Work alone is not justified by any means. We have discussed this already. It is absolutely necessary that wherever we offer training, there must also be artistic and world experience.

Comment. I was reminded of your remark this morning that the threefold order would emerge as if by magic through our working within ourselves, by deepening our understanding of threefold man, and not by trying to impose a threefold order on our surroundings. I think equally it would be dangerous to direct any activity towards overcoming the type, or healing the imbalance in our young people; rather we should direct efforts towards ourselves, towards overcoming our own imbalances. I have had the impression again and again that you have to digest every single thing before it is passed on to the young people; the work you do in the workshop—everything—is digested completely before it goes to the young people.

Comment. When the question arose as to what one should do in the training centres with regard to the mask, it struck me that one cannot possibly change that mask; even an endeavour to do so can only be an illusion. Perhaps one might be permitted the thought that the mask be used to advantage rather than otherwise. To take an example from the realm of the temperaments. The phlegmatic temperament can always show in two quite different directions. It could show by someone putting himself to bed and never getting up again, but also by a certain slowness which allows him to take on a task and then persevere to the very end. We can never hope to turn the water element into the air element; we can only foster the side which is the positive one. We cannot model our own ideas into the mask, but we can build up the image of the mask so that we can see it work. This begins at the stage of puberty. Before puberty we might try to intervene. The moment the mask begins to form we should observe. It is good to recognize the mask as early as possible, and then form the image which can serve as a picture.

Dr. König. I have to add something to the question whether in our training centers we can still try to heal the imbalance of the mask. To try to alter it is wrong. We are not permitted to do it. The doctor may do it because it is part of his job. But it is not part of the job of those who are responsible for the training in the villages. We must now learn that the villagers are entrusted to us with their full karma and that what we were permitted to do before they reached maturity we are not any longer permitted to do afterwards. So if you say 'we cannot' you are right—with the exception that the doctor can.

Question. I have not quite understood the idea of the *Leitbild*. Do these images of humanity arise out of a good imitation or study of what you have developed during these three days?

Dr. König. You should not connect it with a special person. You should try to understand threefold man by means of these three female images, of the three male images—by means of what Rudolf Steiner, Kolisko, and others have worked out concerning threefoldness; but you should not impose it on your fellow man. You can impose it on yourself, but you should not say: 'Oh he is this and therefore we have to do that'. To do so would be entirely wrong; you must leave the other one free. But you should turn inward and build up these images, and let them work. . . . I think you should now simply take this and make your own observations and then in a year come again and we will go on.

Comment. I would like to thank Dr. König. Yesterday he led us into the meditative communion with the spirit, through his description of light and shadow—today he has led us into the glory and manifoldness of what appears spread out before the senses. If we could take with us, not as a memory but as a continuing activity within our soul, the two ways he has led us—if we would learn in our meeting with the villagers to know these two ways and to exercise them—we would make a step forward. I have rarely met the essence of the possibilities that are given to the human spirit upon earth more intensely, more clearly, and more beautifully than in these last two lectures.

The Threefold Constitution of Man

Second Conference
Held in the Camphill Hall, Murtle Estate, Aberdeen, Scotland.
29th January–1st February 1963

Chairman's Opening Remarks

Peter Roth

Given on the evening of 29th January 1963

Dear friends and dear Dr. König,

I would like to welcome you all very warmly. Last year we had our first Village Conference. We met then in a special way, looking forward to the three days of being together with tremendous relief and great joy. To me it appeared then that we had come together out of the storm-tossed seas of village existence to an island of light and peace for the first time.

This time I have quite a different feeling, which is connected with the way those three days last year have worked into the life of our various villages and have permeated them. When we meet now in this Camphill Hall, still surrounded by the light of the Holy Nights, we are graced to experience a kind of Christmas event in contrast to the summer existence of our village life with its immersion into the toil and sweat of the outer world, and our being drawn into differentiation and outer sense experience. Coming together here, away from the humdrum life of our villages, we experience a Christmas of knowledge giving perspective to our problems, tasks and possibilities.

Introduction

Karl König

Given immediately following the Chairman's Opening Remarks

Dear Friends,

I don't think much need be added to the welcome Peter has expressed. The memories of the days which we spent together last year are still very vivid, because, dear friends, last year considerable grace was granted us in our effort to become conscious for the first time of what we do when working in our villages. Some of you may remember that at the opening I had this to say: "We have worked for seven years and it is only now that we meet together for the first time in order to become conscious of what we do", and I actually used the words, "Now we start to go to school."

So today we say to ourselves: 'This year we enter the second year of school.' Whether every one of you has been promoted to this second year or not I don't know: it depends on your own conscience, on whether you have worked on the content of last year's conference wherever you were. I remember very well a discussion between Peter and myself several months ago, in which he thought we should not have a conference this year because of the Movement Council and the Agricultural Conference. He thought next year would be time enough. But it is not good, dear friends, to go to Class 1 for two consecutive years. So my impression is that it is quite right that we meet again in order to continue our work. And let me add that I think it would be necessary to meet again next year if circumstances permit—we should certainly try to meet three times.

ot too many new things will be mentioned in my lectures this time. I will try not to go further than is demanded by the work which you have begun—and in some places have already done very well, I think, and very thoroughly. Nothing especially new will be added, but I will simply try to unfold the three themes which we began to discuss together last year.

Since last year, a great change has taken place within the Camphill Movement; a change which permits us to meet together here in this Hall.* This is an outer sign for what has happened within the whole of the Movement and I can well understand what Peter alluded to in his introduction. What he said could perhaps also be expressed in the following way. Last year our conference was still a kind of family affair. Now it grows into a realm of objectivity, and I very much hope that this level of objectivity will be maintained throughout these three days. I don't mean the objectivity of modern science. What I mean is a sphere of objectivity before the spirit, in such a way, however, that anyone who wishes can listen to what we say. It is not merely small talk which concerns us: it is something which is going to make an imprint on the village impulse throughout the world, because the village impulse has not only taken root in the Camphill Movement but elsewhere too. It started here, but it is now practised far and wide in many different forms. Our task, therefore, is a most important one, dear friends. We have to keep this impulse spiritually abreast of the spiritual tasks of our time.

Perhaps this is a kind of introduction. I think I will have to refer time and again to this objectivity which has now entered into the Village Movement, because otherwise we will be suffocated by the great number of efforts, trials and possibilities which spring up in the world today. I feel it is a most earnest task which lies before us, and if Peter, perhaps quite rightly, has called it a Christmas event, let us also have it not as a family Christmas, but as a Christmas event in the true sense of the word. I hope this will be possible.

---

* The first Camphill Hall dedicated at Michaelmas 1962.

First Lecture

Karl König

Given on the morning of 30th January 1963

Dear Friends,

Looking back to all the knowledg and insight which we gained last year, I think it is necessary to recall the main points in what we were able to work out together. Before doing so, however, let us remind ourselves of the fact that last year we decided in common that the knowledge which we gain, the insight which we increasingly receive, should remain ours at least for the time being. We should not lightheartedly dissipate it, or share it with just anybody who is curious to know what is going on among us. I also have the impression that what we are now going to work out together should remain ours for a certain time. However, it would be wrong of you to interpret this as meaning that it should be a secret; by no means. But things are so tender, dear friends, that I feel only now, after all of you (or many of you) have started to work on the content of last year's conference, is this content able to face the world. And perhaps in a year's time what we are now going to discuss together will also be able to face the world—to be free. I would like you to take in this sense what I am going to say, or better, what I will try to express. Again it will be a struggle, dear friends, again it will be difficult to coin the right phrases, to use the right words, because it is exceedingly subtle to formulate certain ideas for the first time, but nonetheless I consider it imperative for the village impulse, for the work with the villagers. Let me repeat: only if we come to accept the attitude that not everybody, at least not to begin with, can eat this morsel of food which we are preparing together, only then will this food remain a nourishment and a help for many.

There were mainly three things which we tried to understand last year. First, the problem of the *mask*. We began to see our villagers, our young friends, in such a way that we learned to understand that they wear what we called 'masks of humanity'. Because they have such difficulty in establishing their own individuality and personality, they have to wear a mask. We spoke more or less extensively about this and also about various types of mask. We began to recognize the various masks which we could find in works of literature, in life and so on.

The second item was our concern with Rudolf Steiner's picture, 'Light and Shadow', where we tried to understand the more *luciferic and the more ahrimanic side of existence*. I pointed out that what is indicated in the blue face belongs more to the nervous system, whereas the other face, the red face, represents the being of the soul. This soul being finds difficulty in entering into the body; it mirrors itself in the nervous system, and in between the two something new emerges.

The third thing was the *threefold constitution of man on the one hand and woman on the other*—indications which we also tried to take further. I hope that you found them valuable for your understanding of man.

These were the three main chapters which we discussed. But there was something else which I personally consider to be the most important insight we gained last year. It is what I would like to call a 'decision' which we made together, realizing that it is not for us to judge the young villagers, to try to understand why they are as they are. In other words, it is not our task to formulate a diagnosis about and upon them. This means that we are not their judges—be it psychologically, medically, or in any other way—but that our main task is to create within us what we called *Leitbilder*, leading images. This gradual accumulation of leading images within our soul makes it possible for our friends, the villagers, to mirror themselves in these *Leitbilder*, in these images. So it is not we who judge them, it is they who judge themselves—partly consciously, but mainly subconsciously—in such a way that we walk among them having something in us, building up the right leading images in our soul, so that by means of this they are able to begin to recognize themselves. You can see, dear friends, that this is something entirely different from the task of the teacher, and that of the curative teacher. If we work in our villages we will have to more and more overcome the teacher and the curative teacher in us—not to mention the psychologist in us and the medical doctor in us! These attitudes would be quite inappropriate in the working and living together with our villagers, although very valuable in other fields of existence.

But where the village impulse is to be carried, those who would carry it must become (to use a particular, special word) 'shepherds'. And if I say 'shepherds', I do not in the least mean we have to become priests. That is the task of others, but not our task. To become a 'shepherd' means that by one's simple presence the few which have to be led gather around and become peaceful: through our existence they gain certainty within and for themselves. It would be fatal, dear friends, if we did not gradually learn that it is not I who is the 'shepherd' but rather it is these leading images within my soul that are the shepherding power which guides, leads, forms and works. So in this way we are carriers—as we always are—of something that should work through us. I know that this is a long, hard way to go. Some will achieve it; others will not be able to achieve it. But the attempt must be made. And it must be renewed time and again, because only by our becoming 'shepherds', in the way in which I have tried to explain, will something happen which is so vital and so necessary for those—whom I would never like to call the sheep, if by that you were to understand it as looking down—who are entrusted to our care. But our young friends need something. They need—and again I refer to what we tried to understand last year—they need what we call in German *Sicherheit*. I would like to write it down in the following way so that you understand what I mean: *S—ich—erheit*. The word *ich* (I) is contained in this word *Sicherheit* which you can translate as 'security' or 'certainty'; you can also call it 'safety'. If you try to understand what is meant by such words, you can perhaps understand the following. To achieve security, dear friends, means to insert one's ego into one's environment; it means to rest secure within one's own individuality, to be able to go along with one's ego. You will perhaps understand if I say that no animal ever experiences this certainty, security. Every animal's inner soul experience is built on fear, anxiety, joy and happiness. But certainty, security, safety—*Sicherheit*—does not exist, because it is entirely an ego-experience which only human beings can have. *Security, dear friends, is the insertion of our ego in the world around us*: when we are inserted into things in such a way that the window and the ceiling, the chairs and tables, the trees and clouds are ours. This means that we are in them. Then we feel secure; we experience security. As soon as we cannot see properly, cannot hear properly, cannot smell in the right way—as soon as our senses are disturbed or distorted in one way or another—our feeling of security is diminished. It can also be the sense of movement or the sense of touch, or it can be that the arrangement of our senses is such as to make it impossible for our ego to insert itself into the world. As soon as something in this realm is disturbed, insecurity sets in.

There is also a further aspect, namely the relation of our ego to the body: *I, myself, within my body*. If this is established, *I experience certainty*. I am inserted. I am certain; sure of myself. I know how to use my fingers, how to judge the distance, the step, the lightness or heaviness, of myself. My mobility, as long as it is mine, gives me the certainty of my existence. And as long as we are secure and certain, we experience safety; we are safe. To meditate on such an experience, dear friends, will at once open the door for us to a first understanding of what the ego in reality is. And if I were to try to short-cut everything concerning the work in our villages, I would say: Whatever you do should concern itself first of all with an attempt to understand the 'I am'. Don't think that you will ever achieve this: we can only do so when we die, and even then it is not easy. But we should try to approach and to wrestle continually with this question of the 'I' in man. Only if we continually try to do this will we be able to give a feeling of security to those whose 'I' is not able to insert itself completely and fully; thereby we help them nevertheless to feel certain and safe around us. I hope, dear friends, that you can follow so far.

The understanding of this two-fold existence of the ego in man— in security with the world, in certainty within the human body—

already paves the way to an understanding of one of the fundamental truths of this problem: namely to see that on the one hand it creates consciousness, or better, 'it is consciousness', and on the other hand 'it is will'. The great question of what is consciousness and what is will can only be answered if the identification of the 'I' with consciousness and will is encountered. This is the first thing which we must begin to understand because leading images will be created out of it—leading images which will give us again the possibility of approaching the mask. Whenever I go around our villges and meet our young friends, more and more I learn to see them, and I experience them, not as individualities, but as types; types of the wide variety of all humanity: types of tribes, of peoples, of nations, of masses. These types are masks: they wear masks which others have gradually overcome.

Consciousness

Will

Illustration 7

We should now ask a question which so far we have omitted, because it might have been too difficult. We should now ask ourselves for the first time: What is the meaning of the mask which even today people still think is necessary to wear at fancy dress balls, or during *Carnival* in the Rhineland, Basel and other places? If you have ever experienced this—the huge, grotesque masks which people wear—you will understand that here is something which is very strange. Then there are also, for instance, masks which people wear in south eastern Europe during the Holy Nights, when they roam through the villages singing, shouting and displaying gruesome types of faces. What does all this mean? When you enquire into, or try to trace back, this 'custom' (which is quite a wrong word), you will find that wherever humanity appears masks come into being. One could say that the further back we go into pre-historic times, the more important becomes the use of masks. There is no tribe of primitive people which does not use masks at certain special moments in its life: masks during the rites when young people gain manhood, masks during warfare, masks in performing on the stage or in the open air. For many different occasions the leading people wear masks: they dance in masks, they perform their rites in masks, they call upon rain or thunder covered by masks. It is one of the most wonderful pursuits to study the differentiation of masks throughout world history right back to the time of ancient Greece, when tragedies and comedies were performed on huge stages in front of tens of thousands of people by masked actors. There is no doubt, dear friends (and this is now generally known) that the appearance of the mask goes right back to the origin of cults and rites. Wherever primitive cults, wherever primitive rites are performed, it is not the individual person who enacts it, but the masked one. And those who wear the mask are, in wearing it, endowed with the powers which the mask represents. This means that if, for instance, a tribe understands or believes that the jaguar is its leading spirit, the sorcerer, the medicine man, wears the mask of the jaguar at special moments, and thereby invokes the power of this being to descend and permeate him. The mask is, so to speak, the focal point around which spiritual powers can gather. But the individual hides behind the mask. There are certain tribes—many in the Congo, and also in North America—where during the initiation rites of puberty, when a boy grows into manhood, the following is enacted. Suddenly, in the course of their rituals, masked figures appear and aggress the young boys whose task is now to fight back and to tear off the mask, in order to discover that they are among people. The ego may hide behind the mask, but it is also a task to destroy the mask so that the individual can appear. So there is always this conflict between the mask and the individuality. The individuality recedes behind the mask. The individuality also tries to destroy the mask to, as it were, rend the curtain of the mask in twain. It is the ultimate de-masking when the curtain in the temple of Jerusalem is rent in twain, because then the ego of the world appears in the realm of mankind.

Having come this far, dear friends, we still have to ask ourselves: What is the mask? Are we at all able to find the archetypal image of the mask, the *Ur-bild*? I think we can, because as soon as I say that the Sphinx is the archetype of every mask, you will understand what I mean. Rudolf Steiner once spoke about the Sphinx in the following way. He described how in Atlantean times the human bodily form was still animal-like with a receding forehead, a protruding chin, huge teeth. We saw each other like this in early Atlantean times, when we met during the day. In Lemurian times we were endowed with wings and claws that were even more animal-like. But when in Atlantean times we met during the night, we discovered that above this animal-like body the ideal form of the human ego and countenance appeared in etheric structure. In connection with this Rudolf Steiner goes on to say the following:

> Now imagine this memory of the old Atlantean conscious-ness put before man in a symbolic way in Egyptian times. Imagine, the Egyptian priest wanted to say to his people: In Atlantean times your own souls, when they were awake, saw the human form in animal shape—yet at night there arose a beautiful human head. This memory, plastically metamorphosed in sculpture, is the Sphinx.[11]

Rudolf Steiner explains here that in Egyptian times the memory of these Atlantean experiences was put before man in the form of the Sphinx: an animal body, wing-like arms, claws, lion-like legs, but a human face appearing out of this animal existence; the ego appearing through the form of the forehead.

If we learn to understand this as a leading image, and carry it within us, we will learn to understand what the mask means in reality. All the other masks are just parts, parcels, bits and pieces of the one great Sphinx. The Sphinx represents the power of the four great beings of the Zodiac—the Lion, Bull, Waterman and Eagle. When we wear masks we invoke the spiritual powers of all the signs of the Zodiac. True masks represent the different powers of the Zodiac. Masks appear in animal form because it is the Zodiac, the *Tierkreis*, which they represent. Gradually the ego appears, shedding the mask, and man becomes an individual. Do hold fast to these two possibilities—the ego in the centre, fighting the masks, either hiding behind or revealing itself beyond the mask.

There is a grandiose piece of art in which this is expressed in the most beautiful way. It is the second movement of Beethoven's fourth piano concerto. In it you will experience the struggle of the ego against the mask. The piano displays the subtle, soft power of the ego; the orchestra, representing the might of the mask, continually tries to overpower the piano. Gradually the ego increasingly becomes the ruler of the situation, and then everything is dissolved in glory. I don't know whether any of you remembers this. I advise you to listen to it as often as possible.

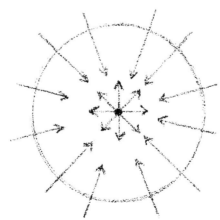

This is the "Tierkreis" . . . . the Ego in the centre . . . .

Illustration 8

Let us take a step further, by going back into the history of masks. Before they were formed—out of wood, metal, stone, clay, hair and all kinds of materials—before they were used, and even at the time they first appeared, something else was done in order to be masked: one painted over one's body and face. Some scientists think that covering the body with paint preceded the mask. Maybe—maybe not. I have no decided view on this. You have probably seen pictures of face and body painting which is still practised by many primitive tribes. Also in 'tribes' of very civilized people much is being tried by way of painting. Something is achieved by this means which is connected with the mask: either to hide, or to pronounce. You either wish to draw attention to your finger nails, or you try to hide behind a mask of paint. I remember a story illustrating the effectiveness of such painting. A German cavalry officer said to his friend: "I bet you I can ride naked through the streets of our little city in broad daylight and nobody will notice." And so he did, completely painted over in the colours of the uniform, and nobody noticed. It is quite amazing what can be done with paint. But also with body painting an attempt is made to evoke the spirit. You may perhaps remember how a victorious soldier in ancient Rome led his triumphant army into Rome, painted over with cinnabar in order to represent Jupiter (Zeus). But painting and mask lead to something else—and this is difficult to express because there is no English word which really describes it. This is what in German is called *Schmuck*. If you look it up in the dictionary, you will find many words: ornament, decoration, jewellery, adornment, finery, attire, embellishment. All is covered by the one word *Schmuck*. But *Schmuck* itself does not exist in English, because English is a language lacking *Schmuck*, lacking adornment. I mean this quite seriously. You see, the best word in English to cover all this would be 'fancy', but 'fancy' already implies something which is not included in the word *Schmuck*. *Schmuck* is everything which adorns the human body: dresses, pendants, rings, chains, any silver, gold, copper, tin or precious stones, and much besides made of wood or any other materials; all this is *Schmuck*. It is not only jewellery, not only finery, not only embellishment; it is all and everything that human beings wore—and this is most interesting, dear friends—*before* they clothed themselves.

So first we have the mask. Then we have adornment. And only finally we have dress and clothing. I must mention this although you might ask why do I talk about such things? You want to know something about our villagers, and I talk about adornment! But we have to understand that to wear adornments is entirely different from wearing a mask. If you try to experience within yourself what it means to put on a ring, a tie-pin or cuff-links or something of that nature—I speak now of my own experience—you will immediately feel that your own personality, your ego, is concerned with its own value here on earth. You feel a certain satisfaction when you have something like jewellery to wear. If you see little children adorning themselves, embellishing themselves (especially girls) you will immediately understand that they reassure themselves of their own value, their own individuality, their own existence, by doing it. It is one of the most important things in education to help one's own children to appear neat and proper, because to have, for instance, a proper frock or a nice hat or new shoes—even a ring—establishes the value of one's own individuality. This is not all fancy, not even for the consciousness soul. The consciousness soul, too, needs such things. Even in the animal kingdom you find traces of this. Did you know, for instance, that male penguins walk along the beach looking for a beautifully coloured pebble, which they pick up and put in front of their chosen one, and she accepts it? It is wonderful to see such a gesture. Did you also know that in a certain type of pigeon, in which the female has blue eyes, the male picks blueberries in order to offer it as a gift for their incipient wedding? Such things do exist. I would not say that this is done consciously or that the ego does it. But in man something develops through the experience of all this 'fancy', 'finery', 'embellishment', 'adornment'. To wear a bracelet, to wear headgear, or to wear any kind of adornment revalues our own personality, and this is necessary for our life and existence. If you ask the question: If the Sphinx is the archetypal image for the mask, where do we find the archetypal image of adornment, of finery, of jewellery? then I would have to say the 'sacrificial stone', the altar, is the archetypal image of every kind of adornment, because wth the altar-stone on which we sacrifice we adorn the piece of ground where we are going to pray, where we are going to celebrate, where we are going to sacrifice. And from primeval times onward, if we wear any kind of adornment we simply show that we communicate with the powers of the world. But we no longer communicate with the Zodiac; we now communicate with the whole world of the planets. In their courses they form the rings and emblems around us, around our bodies—and we receive, as it were, the value of our existence by the courses of the moving stars.

It is therefore not surprising that to make jewellery and adornment became a special undertaking of man at the time metals were discovered, because then form and material came into their own: iron and Mars, lead and Saturn, tin and Jupiter, gold and the Sun, silver and the Moon, and so on. Let me say: 'The world now begins to adorn its own image which appeared in the form of man.' I have described this in such detail because precisely here lies one of the main spheres where our villagers may find their occupation, may find their own work. They will show you that they are able to do it. Not piecework, but adornment in every possible way, wherever you can bring it about.

So first the mask, then adornment, and now the third, which is clothing—the clothes, the dress, which men and women wear. This is the last step. First we had masks. Secondly the world adorned our bodies with adornments. And lastly we began to wear clothes. It is not because it was cold that we tried to cover ourselves. Only zoologists believe this, although no animal, as far as I know, wears any kind of clothing. They accustom themselves in a different way to different climates. Man began to experience his nakedness and this nakedness was experienced not as male, but as female. In the rites and cults of primitive people it was always the male who was the bearer of the mask, while in every rite and cult the female appeared naked but covered with jewellery. For the Hindu, for instance, it is still the case today that to him a naked woman means the revelation of *Prakriti*, and *Prakriti* is the all-prevailing power of life and existence. With the embellishment of adornment—with the rising power of the ego—nakedness becomes conscious, and human beings began to cover the naked body. Before, the body was not perceived s naked. What then reveals the archetypal image of all clothing? It is the grave. When the grave rises above the ground as a mound, tumulus or pyramid, it becomes the house, the temple and the cathedral. Architecture and clothing (dressmaking) are very closely connected. The roots of both are the same. I am sorry to say so, but it is true. What the architect does for the earth, the dressmaker does for man. Not that a suit is a beautiful cathedral now—we are very far from that. It is not even a hall any more. Nevertheless, the roots are the same.

If you now consider the mask, if you consider adornment, and if you consider clothing—you are considering the three aspects of the ego: the ego fighting with the powers of the Zodiac; the ego endowed by and playing with the powers and forces of the planetary world; the ego enshrined in the powers of the earth, the tomb of the earth. We have to consider these three steps, whether we like it or not, because we see them daily before us in our young friends. How and in which way we can leave to our discussion and to what I will try to say tomorrow. But you will understand what I pointed out to you at the start of today's lecture, namely how subtle and how tender all this is, what a beginning it is, and therefore how tenderly we should treat it.

Discussions with Dr. König

Question. When you spoke about clothing, I was reminded of the story of Adam and Eve and the appearance of man. I wondered how to relate that to what you described?

Dr. König. It is the awakening of the ego, accompanied by the experience of nakedness. This is an image, of course, that we read in the Bible. It is a symbolic way of expressing what happened then. Man did not look at all as he looks now.

Question. I wanted to ask about the relationship of the mask to adornment and clothing. You pointed out how in earlier civilizations, and even today in primitive peoples, the mask is put on for the purpose of endowing the individual with the power of a spiritual being. How does this relate to ornaments and clothes? These two things are much more individual, whereas the mask is something above the individual. You also mentioned in a slightly different connection the wearing of uniforms. To me it appears that the mask endows a group of individuals with the presence of a higher being, whereas this does not seem to be so with the other two.

Dr. König. For deductive purposes I had to speak about the mask and then jewellery, finery and all that, and in the end about clothing. But in point of fact these three cannot be seen together in the same way as the threefold human being. I will try to speak about this tomorrow. There are elements of the mask in jewellery, in adornment and in clothing. For instance, if you put on a uniform you draw a mask, as it were, over the clothing. But you can also wear completely unmasked clothing, which you do if you put on what are called 'civvies'; then there is no element of the mask in it. With jewellery, if an emperor wears a crown it is already a mask—at least there is an element of the mask in it—but if it is a single ring, there is no mask. These three elements continually weave into one anoter. There are other differences. In the mask it is always the battle between the ego and the powers of the universe. Whether these universal powers are invoked or are overcome doesn't matter; it is the ego which is there. With jewellery it is not so much the ego: the ego feels something in wearing jewellery; it is satisfied—but what actually expresses itself in jewellery is the astrality of the world interacting (in work, in play) with one's own astrality. And when we wear clothing, we give expression to the different forms of our etheric body, so that clothing 'is' the etheric body; jewellery 'is' the astral body; mask 'is' the ego. But they also belong together: they are one, just as the upper, the middle and the lower part of man are integrated.

Question. I wondered about how the mask, adornment and clothing are worn? The mask is mainly worn where the head is; and adornment at the special point of transition—chest or neck; whilst clothing covers the whole body.

Dr. König. This is a most important point. I will speak about this tomorrow and then go one step further. You cover one expression of the individuality when you wear a mask; everything else is bare, but the face is overcome. All kinds of adornment are always worn where the rhythmical organization—heart and breath—meet. And clothing applies in the metabolic-limb area.

Comment. I always thought of clothing as an expression of the way the ego incarnates into the human being throughout the centuries.

Dr. König. Does not the ego work on the etheric? I would not say that every year's fashions are an expression of the ego—but in the course of the centuries the ego, incarnating step by step, changes the structure of the etheric.

Comment. I am taken by the picture of the ego which tears down the mask and on the other hand uses the mask. On the blackboard you sketched consciousness and will. During the last year in the village there were one or two occasions which puzzled me, because something happened among villagers which I could not explain as a result of their consciousness. It was an action which one would expect to be called forth rather by conscience. I perceived also an element of tearing down the mask. We create and follow the rhythm of our daily life, and with the ego active in this way in the will sphere, we help the other aspect of the ego which has to do with conscience rather than with consciousness. As an example I could cite the following: Rosalind was away for a few days. Our married couple, Mary and Jim, looked after the house; Mary was cooking. When the Sunday lunch was over, the 'phone rang, and Mary ran to it. One of the other villagers had called to ask, "Can I cook the supper for you?" That is the kind of thinking which we bring about only with a certain amount of struggle. But I regard this as conscience.

Dr. König. I very much doubt whether to ascribe this to conscience. I would rather suggest that our young friends have a much wider consciousness than we have, because their egos are not yet as hard and firmly incarnated as ours. And you know psychologists of today quite rightly speak of the narrowness of our consciousness. But by growing narrower our consciousness becomes lighter and lighter within its narrow focus. In former times it was much wider. Gradually our consciousness became narrower and narrower; we lost almost every supersensible experience, and now we wear, so to speak, blinkers. The consciousness of our villagers is wider and so they can still sense: 'It is too much for Mary so I'm going to help her.'

Question. Is it perhaps true that this kind of extended consciousness is one of the elements that bring about the tolerance our villagers have?

Dr. König. The extended consciousness makes tolerance possible. *We* are not tolerant; we are even very intolerant. Tolerance comes out of an entirely different realm of the soul than consciousness: open up that realm and tolerance might flow.

Comment. Adornment, as I understand it, also has something to do with symbols. It des happen that these symbols are misused. The Swastika is taken from the Germanic Sun-worship. It is a symbol which calls upon the emotions powerfully.

Dr. König. This helps you understand the power of such a symbol.

Comment. A striking example of what you say is the Highland dress, the tartan plaid and kilt. It is said that the colours of the tartan arose from the faculty of the clairvoyant highlander to see the colours of the person before him. They tried to retain the colours of the clans in the Highland dress.

Dr. König. The basic colour in the highland dress is green. The different shades and forms are fancy. Green is nothing else but the after-image of the colour of the blood. They then tried to embellish this, to assert their own inner light. Perhaps they did not see all this; but in some way through experience it arose.

Comment. I would like to say something about adornment and clothing. You mentioned that we should try to make adornment available to the villagers to give them the possibility of establishing this realm within themselves. In this connection we tried to look at clothing. We concerned ourselves with the question: What kind of dress could one wear in this or that profession? We tried to add some adornment to enliven it's utility. National dress seems hardly appropriate; in putting on national dress you connect yourself wrongly with the national spirit. But as we are such a mixed crowd, we don't even know from where to take the adornment. We always come back to the individual, seeking what he or she would require in this or that profession or craft.

Dr. König. It would be quite undesirable if a kind of uniform emerged in our villages because you would enhance the power of the mask. Not to mention national costume! What a terrible thought! Imagine if we were to suddenly wear Highland dress, or run about in kilts. It would be quite wrong. What we have to do is to strengthen the individual. I do not mean to strengthen the individual dress, the general wear, the daily cardigans, kirts, or blouses. They are so ugly that one can hardly stand them. Let us learn to dress the individual beautifully. This can only happen if a certain amount of taste appears. Then we will learn how to beautify the dress. I even doubt whether one should wear different clothes for the different crafts, unless they are utility clothes. Nothing unified—no 'arts and crafts'!

Comment. In regard to crafts or other work activities, I have always stressed that one should wear clothes expressive of what one is doing. I still feel that this is true. It helps villagers more than anything else to recognise themselves because the mask becomes visible mask—and the activity in the workshop or farm is something which I feel becomes more conscious for them if they do wear the appropriate clothing.

Comment. I think this is very important. I have no doubt that one is helped to do one's work properly when one is dressed for the particular occasion. I see the danger to which you have pointed in our feeling that we must invent work clothes anew on the basis of medieval forms. For example, Mr. Will the plumber, has done a training, and therefore he wears a different pair of overalls from all the other plumbers. We might take this up and modify it to make it appropriate for our setting in a modern way, instead of bringing up a Romanesque past. Our tendency to hanker after the beauty of the past is wrong even if the Romanesque period seems to us more attractive than the present. But that is not helpful. Our resistance to the fashion of today and our preference for the one of five years ago is no spiritual advance.

Dr. König. I fully agree—if it does not go beyond that.

Question. I have a more general question in connection with mask, adornment and clothing. It is the question of beauty. It has already been mentioned that in various ages and civilizations the clothing has varied a great deal, but as in adornment, the very idea is one of beauty. If one studies the masks, though, one is struck by the preponderance of ugliness; it is the ugliness which is usually accentuated. Why is there this discrepancy between the ugliness of the mask and the beauty of the other two areas?

Dr. König. Tomorrow morning I will answer this question.

Second Lecture

Karl König

Given on the morning of 31st January 1963

Dear Friends,

Today we will continue with our theme. What we embark on will be even more subtle than the rather 'ornamental' descriptions we used yesterday. Mask, adornment and clothing are something we can still hold on to; something to which we are more or less accustomed, and which we have tried to understand. I hope that yesterday morning's deliberations made clear the importance of our attitudes toward mask, adornment and clothing. These attitudes appeared almost from the beginning, when man started to tread the ground of this earth, which means from the moment when, during the time of Lemuria, the first human beings (Adam and Eve) found themselves in a more or less physical existence. We should, however, make quite clear to ourselves that masks, adornment and clothing do not come to man from without. They were not introduced, produced, or brought about because men and women felt alone here on earth, or because they were shivering with cold, or experienced fear and shame. It is certainly connected with all that, but it is an inherent tendency of the human soul to wear masks, to put on jewellery, adornment of any kind, and to dress. Will you please hold fast to this: that it is a tendency of the human soul.

Many things contribute to this tendenc. No doubt even shivering with cold, and also fear and shame, flow into it, as well as the soul's recognition of the wonders and the manifoldness of the world around her. Yet there are these three fundamental tendencies of the human soul which express themselves, first, in the wearing of a mask. Whether he mask unites the leader of the tribe with the ancestral being of that tribe or whether it unites him with the divine powers, it is the tendency of the soul to hide behind a mask. The second tendency of the soul is to wear adornment, jewellery, finery, and by so doing to establish its own value and dignity. I am not speaking about modern ways of wearing jewellery, or wearing masks: I remain with the archetypal images. The third tendency is to dress, to veil, and thereby to attain to something much larger. To be veiled is entirely different from hiding. To be veiled is to put oneself as a soul in the position of being buried here on earth. Dear friends, I point this out because my impression is that it is so very important that you, who have to deal with villagers, more and more obtain a real feeling, a real impression, of the higher being of man—the human soul. Now what I would like to offer to you this morning is not a great deal, but I will try to ensure that it reaches you with the intensity which is due it. We should learn to understand that it is the soul which manifests these three tendencies. And to enquire into this will be our morning's aim.

What in point of fact are these tendencies? When we speak about the human soul, we must realise at once that the soul is not only a being here on earth between birth and death, but that the soul is also a being dwelling in the spiritual world between death and rebirth. So whenever we imagine the soul we have to learn that it has an existence which comes and goes before our inner eyes, like a kind of breathing: a breathing which goes from birth to death, and from death to birth. This is the human soul. There is nothing which needs to be added at this point. The human soul is a 'Beinghood': irrespective of here or there, of birth or death, of living in this realm or in yonder realm.

Illustration 9

To doubt, to neglect, or to discount this, even to forget it again every day, takes something away from our 'shepherd' existence. For where shall our young friends gain their certainty and security if we are not continually aware of and count on this indestructibility of the human soul which here *(see Illustration 9)*, going from birth to death, is inhaled and there, going from death to rebirth, is exhaled? We need not talk about it, and we should also not assert that it is so, but we should learn to wake up in the morning knowing that a small, a tiny inhaling of my soul has taken place, and we should go to sleep knowing clearly and definitely that now my soul experiences a small exhaling, because this process which from birth to death is a great inhaling, is daily and nightly a small inhaling and a small exhaling. You will say, 'But we do this anyway', and I must reply, 'Yes, but we always forget it'. So my question is (and I put it to you again): Where would our villagers find their certainty and security—in the sense in which I pointed to certainty and security yesterday—and thereby breathe, if this experience were not our daily bread? A very short prayer: I exhale my soul into the spirit. I inhale my soul. The experiencing of this coming and going should be of the greatest importance to us.

But if within yourself you try to discover what takes place when you exhale, and what takes place when you inhale: what this simple breathing process is—this daily process of 'birth' and 'death', or the greater process of birth and death—you will then find underlying it three tendencies within the human soul. I am not speaking about the human ego; I am speaking about the human soul. We must learn to distinguish between the ego and soul in the same way in which we tried to distinguish yesterday between mask and adornment.

We will now consider this from quite a different point of view. These three tendencies can be expressed in the following way. (Rudolf Steiner gave certain lectures in 1921, called *Fundamentals of Occult Psychology*,[12] which I would very strongly recommend all of you to study, especially in connection with your work). Rudolf Steiner describes how in the human soul there is the tendency on the one hand to become world and on the other hand to become man. Becoming world, growing out of oneself—in terms of ordinary breathing we could also say 'exhaling'—is uniting oneself with everything that is both here on earth in the world of the senses, and over there in the supersensible world of the spirit. In the spiritual world it is a uniting of oneself with those to whose karma we are bound; a uniting with angelic and archangelic beings; with the cosmic script, with the cosmic sound, with the cosmic word. It is becoming world: exhaling. On the other hand becoming man is turning again to oneself; is inhaling, reflecting, trying to establish oneself. And then, in the equilibrium between ecoming world and becoming man, between exhaling and inhaling, the soul experiences herself. These, dear friends, are the three tendencies out of which our soul is woven. I would say the physiology of our soul is contained in these three tendencies. I do not say the 'morphology' of the soul; the substance is somewhat different. But it is not necessary to discuss this at the moment.

Now, dear friends, to try to understand these three tendencies should become a daily task, a daily questioning: Where do we become world, where do we become man and how do we establish ourselves? This will lead to a very first understanding of what is mask and adornment and clothing, because no doubt the mask leads us into becoming world, and good clothing into becoming man. We establish ourselves when we are dressed. We would not dare to meet others naked. Some of us would not even dare to meet themselves naked. I know that many people shy away (sometimes rightly, sometimes not quite rightly) from going around naked even behind locked doors. This is quite different for children. We must learn to dive without any hesitation or shyness into these finer subtleties of the human soul in order to become the 'shepherds' which we are meant to be.

This is what we have to understand first of all. Then however, starting from another direction, we must also learn to understand something else. The human soul not only has these three tendencies, but today the human soul is woven in such a way that into its texture is inserted the possibility to think and the power to will. And feeling arises out of the soul herself when she is penetrated by thinking and willing. I am trying to be as careful as possible, so that the being of the human soul will become ever more tangible. May I repeat (and please forgive me for being so particular) the human soul in her present condition is endowed with the ability to think and the power of will. And in so far as these two existentialities live in the soul, feeling arises like, to take a very simple image, the child arises out of man and wife—if man and wife are able to derstand that the child is not theirs at all but arises out of the common ground whereon they meet each other.

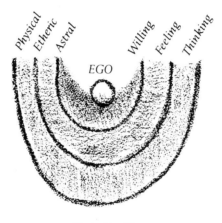

Illustration 10

If we now look at the human being in such a way that we have here *(see Illustration 10)* the physical body, here the etheric body, and here the astral body and the ego (I have not specially chosen the colours I use), then thinking lives in the space between the physical and etheric bodies, feeling lives in the space between the etheric and the astral bodies, and willing livesere between the astral body and the ego. I will partially fill this dot—which indicates the ego—with willing, because the ego is woven out of the substance of the will. If you take all this away, as it were—the etheric, astral and ego—you find yourself still in the sphere of the soul. But here on earth the part of thinking which we bring with us from the world of spirit resides in the hollow space between our physical and etheric body. You will recall how, time and again, Rudolf Steiner has led us deep into the mysteries of human existence, so you will know exactly that we are born out of the spirit and that we take with us the possibility of thinking which has cosmic texture, has cosmically woven thoughts that in themselves are life and power, and that with this we build our body and its organs. We bring this with us at birth, and here on earth it lives between our own ether body and our physical existence.

On the other side of the etheric body which faces the astrality, our soul's existence, there lives feeling. It weaves between the etheric and the astral, as sympathy, antipathy, and as all the different moods which continually permeate us—the moods from the past, the moods from the future—which make up the background colour of our daily life. And then where we ourselves are, where our ego is, the will acts in connection with the soul. Thinking, feeling and willing are again permeated by the three tendencies of the soul: to become world, to become man, and to be man. But these three tendencies are not fixed so that thinking is to become world and willing is to become man. It is different, and with the help of indications which Rudolf Steiner has given I will try to describe how it differs.

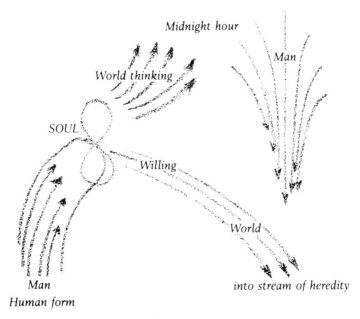

Illustration 11

When we die the soul enters into the realm of spirit, taking with her thinking and willing. Rudolf Steiner describes that after death thinking has the greatest wish to open itself up and become world. We may indicate this in such a way that the thinking now fills the whole world in its tendency to exhale. Willing, however, takes an entirely different direction; it wants to become man; it seeks for the human form. Thus thinking wants to become world; willing wants to become man, and in between there remains the soul. Imagine thinking spreading out and willing tending towards form, and the soul herself remaining. But then comes what Rudolf Steiner calls the 'midnight hour' between death and rebirth, and at this 'midnight hour' the soul decides to return again to earth. In doing so it draws together, inhales, wants to be man, as previously it had wanted to be world. On the other hand, willing, which previously wanted to become man, to become human form, now has the tendency to become world. What does this mean, that willing wants to become world and thinking to become man? It means that thinking already looks towards the coming earth existence, trying to form, not yet the substance, but the image of man. The will, on the other hand, having acquired the human cosmic form, now wants to become world, exhaling and uniting with the hereditary stream. For generations our will lives in the stream of heredity of our forefathers—and only at the moment of conception and birth does it meet and unite with the human form. And then will, having been world, wants to become man; and thinking, which has made man, wants to become world. This already happens here on earth. These are now the smaller, much more subtle breathing processes in willing and in thinking, which the soul bears in herself as a tendency, as continual becoming, continual striving, to become man; clothing, mask, adornment.

But when you look at life on earth, and at how men live and what they try to achieve, you will perhaps find that in our lives there is a kind of, let me say, 'mid-day' hour. As over yonder there is a 'midnight hour', so here there is a 'mid-day' hour. You will observe this especially if you study the great men, who obviously made an impact on and contribution to human existence here on earth. So when we enter into earthly existence, there is in our thinking, which lives between physical and etheric body, the tendency to become world, and in our willing the tendency to become man. The longing to become world is answered, of course, by this huge garment whereby we shared out the golden fleece of our twelve senses. This is, so to speak, the cosmic *Urgewandung* (primal garment) which we carry with us, and through this cosmic primal garment thinking has the possibility to exhale, to become world. And by the staff of our ego, the will becomes man.

But when we grow up—some quicker, some slower, many not at all—those who grow up reach a 'mid-day' hour wherein this tendency is again turned around in such a way that willing now wants to become world, wants to establish itself in the work, in the achievement, in all that men wish to create around them. Whether we like to furnish our room in a special way, or whether we want to write a book or to build an engine, it is our will, with its tendency to become world. When this is done, our thinking reflects, begins to wonder: Who am I? What do I have to do here on earth? The thinking wants to become man. And at the moment when thinking *is* man and willing *is* world, we are at last permitted to put down our tools and die. And then it begins again—that in the spirit-world the tendency of the will turns toward becoming man, and thinking wants t spread out into the world of the spirit, regaining thereby its true power, fullness and quality. All this resides in the soul, dear friends. To put on a mask, to make a mask, is to become world. To put on clothing is to become man. To wear adornment, jewellery, finery, is to *be* man; is to establish one's value and dignity. With this description we have pointed to the three fundamental tendencies of the human soul. As our body lives by in- and exhaling from the moment of birth until the moment of death, so our soul lives eternally in becoming world, in becoming man—in so far as this earth in its roundness is eternal. There are different forms of eternity, but what is meant here is the eternity between the Alpha and the Omega, between the beginning and the end, and this is the eternity of the

becoming Man—becoming world—being Man.

These are the three tendencies of the soul, and we have now heard how these three tendencies make masks and adornment and clothing, so that going one step further we might ask ourselves: Where and what is the substance out of which all this is woven? Certainly it is gold and silver, it is wool and linen, it is hair and straw—and many other things. But from where does it really arise?

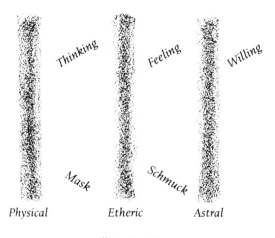

Illustration 12

Dear friends, let us look again at what I tried to point out to you. Let us say *(pointing to Illustration 12)*, that here is the ether body and here the physical body, while here is the astral body, and that in between these lives thinking and feeling and, together with it all, that which appears in adornment, in embellishments; in all kinds of ornaments, precious stones, headgear and so on. It all appears here, for this is the substance out of which it is woven. Our feeling lives in it. If you decorate a glass it takes place here. If you hammer gold, or if you inscribe something, it all arises from here. The being of the mask, however—and I point again to the becoming world with the help of the Golden Fleece of the twelve senses—is here. All our clothing, all our dresses—everything that we wear—are an expression of the form of our etheric body, be it tartan, be it whatever. . . I point this out to you in order that you do not form schemata in your thinking, because if you now seek the ego, you have to find it here and here, all over and throughout *(see Illustration 13)*. This applies to the soul as well, so that willing is here, but also there and there. Looking at it broadly, this is our aim: to make masks, to make adornment, to make clothing.

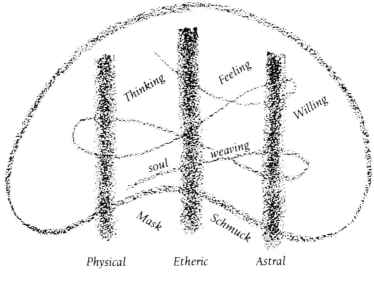

Illustration 13

We shall leave this now. We will discuss it again, and I very much hope that some of you will take it up as the next task, for your work will be to learn to understand what is called ethnology because all this is nothing else but ethnology: how rites and customs, totems and taboos appear in one or another primitive people. These are again leading images whereby we establish our existence as 'shepherds' within our work.

Discussions with Dr. König

Comment. In connection with the mask, I feel that nowadays for so-called normal people a great danger arises of becoming 'psychological masks'. This was not so in former times, and maybe what you call neurosis and such like are a kind of mask in the psychological realm.

Dr. König. It fits exactly with what we tried to indicate last year. Only ordinary people have the tendency and possibility to change their masks or even their one neurosis into another, whereas our villagers keep their mask fixed. This is the only difference. I think we pointed out last year that right up to the Middle Ages and even into our own time—in as far as people still live in the condition of the Middle Ages—every occupation, trade, or craft wore its own mask. The Middle Ages was a time when you could tell exactly that he is a butcher or a shoemaker, he is a tanner, and so on; not only because they were dressed in a special way, but because they also looked their part. Their expression was the mask of their trade. All this has now disappeared of course. You can still sometimes recognise a farmer, or a builder perhaps, but this is just about all. However, new things are more and more taking shape now. I can already distinguish the mask of the motor mechanic, which is quite different from the woodworker, etc.

Comment. Our young people have very fixed masks and we would like to change them because they are something which we do not necessarily want to keep.

Dr. König. Last year we spoke about the mask in today's world. This year we tried to understand the meaning of the mask through the ages, and we found that on the one hand the ego hides behind the mask in order that higher powers can work through it. On the other hand the ego overcomes the mask and breaks through it, as for instance in certain tribal puberty rites, in order that one's own individual countenance can be born. We should create such leading images in us, but we should resist the tendency to change our young friends. We should only have the tendency to alter ourselves. They will accept or not accept—gain or not gain—by what we do within ourselves. As soon as they can mirror themselves in the leading images which we build, a great change will come upon them. In the same way that grass and flowers grow differently on the path by which people walk to and from the church than by a highway or motor road.

Comment. I cannot imagine that the changing of our masks is done differently now from how it will be done in the future. Most people change it through changing their surroundings. That is a power which should actually do it.

Dr. König. It is our ego, because only the ego acquires habits. The ego acquires certain necessary things; morning and evening habits. But it is also able to change its habits again. Who else should do it? The ego is to the astral body as the physical body is to the world. Don't think in rigid concepts, dear friends, concepts which are like separate sticks: one stick for the ego, another stick for the astral body, and a third for the etheric body. They are all working together. How do you imagine an etheric body, an astral body and an ego not interacting once they are together?

Comment. We are still driven too much by our intellectual thinking.

Dr. König. It is your ego which is the driving force. Independence you have anyway.

Question. How often has one got it?

Dr. König. Very, very rarely. But what are we talking about? Our ego is gradually evolving... If you would acquire more now, the whole Jupiter evolution would not be necessary.

Question. Can we extend adornment as far as to include the furniture of one's room; interior decoration?

Dr. König. I think so. The longer you live in a room, the more it becomes your own. It is nothing else but part of your extended body. You can also call a picture or an ornament a personal adornment, if you understand that by it you also increase or assert your own value. We all do this. You simply build something around you in order to experience yourself, be it in the house, or even in the garden—yes, most certainly.

Question. Do you think that what you said in regard to thinking and willing, morning and evening, could be brought together with Rudolf Steiner's lecture on prayer. The question of the religious and spiritual life in the villages is still quite unresolved. I imagine that the breathing which you describe has to do with this question.

Dr. König. I had that lecture on prayer very much in mind when I spoke. I am grateful for what you said because this is one of the fundamentals, like light and shadow.

Question. Could you write a prayer? Something especially for villages?

Dr. König. If you think I could, I could.

Question. I wanted to say something more about what you mentioned yesterday—the possibility of wearing adornment in connection with our villagers. Should one make special things, so that they could see to their own adornment?

Dr. König. I have the impression that work in our village workshops should concentrate on the making of adornment and clothing, rather than anything else, because just in this realm—and I include here many other things—in this realm our handicapped friends could live. As soon as you make mechanical merchandise, you no longer call on their full potential; you simply mechanise the mask. You even mechanise the soul mask. If that is done in other villages, well and good. But I feel that we should keep alive certain tendencies with regard to work. We are gradually developing into a world devoid of adornment, completely devoid of beauty, consisting of little cut-out forms made by the million which everybody has. In an ordinary kind of house you see a door handle which is simply a cranked piece of metal having nothing to do any more with the human hand which grasps it. We should try to keep alive such modes of work which will carry with them powers of life.

You see, dear friends, I am convinced that for instance the toys which we produce in our village at Botton are not only nice but, because they are largely made by hand, they bring soul and life powers to the children who play with them, whether they know it or not. And so it can be with many things—that without talking about it, we send life forces into the world. This is necessary.

Comment. That is also borne out by the necklaces which were a great success with regard to the young people who made them as well as the people who want to have them.

Dr. König. What are we doing when we make necklaces? We go back to an old art, African or American Indian, where you find them beautifully done. They are made out of various seeds and such like. We make them not in order to go back but in order to nourish the soul forces of children, of young people.

Comment. I want to say something more about adornment. You once suggested that we make our children's clothing and everything that pertains to children in our workshops as a right thing to do for our villagers—and toys also belong there. The toy has a special significance for the child—perhaps the same as adornment has later for the older child and the young girl.

Dr. König. We should once seriously discuss in one or two meetings the meaning of toys, materials and so on. It would be very important. To make children's dresses would be excellent. Perhaps you can discover Rudolf Steiner's indications for making them. Then again you will learn how thinking turns to the world, and willing wants to become man. Why don't you start to do such things? There would be a market even in this country, I am convinced. There are hundreds of things which could be made. And you have seen, dear friends, that our villagers can make jewellery quite easily. And certainly toys belong there too.

Comment. There are three things we have to consider. First, is the product we want to make right? Second, can our villagers do it? Third, will it sell? We can only find out by trial and error.

Comment. I once had a pupil to whom I gave a necklace of mine. I saw him ten years later. He said, "I can't produce enough of it."

Dr. König. If we do it in the right way, the stores will accept it. We have to find the right materials, the people who do it—and we have to educate the customer.

Comment. We spoke about the value of adornment and all the forces which live in this sphere. I remember the impressions one can still have if one walks through a medieval town such as still exist today. There live people who still wear their professional mask. Being in such a town creates within you a wealth of joy, happiness and well-being. One meets at every corner these living forces. Probably also our villages will have to become such places again, where these forces can find their home for the future.

Dr. König. But not in a medieval form—in a new form. Imagine for instance the influence of towns like Nürnberg, Florence, etc., where large numbers of tourists stream in and out. This is due to the fact that life forces were at work there in the past. In this connection, may I remind you that when we started our workshops in Newton Dee many years ago, I tried to point out that the morality in the world was decreasing more and more, and that in doing work by

115

hand—in the forest, in the fields, in the shops—moral substance is created? This moral substance streams out into the world together with the life forces. You know, for instance, what influence a shoemaker can have, a dressmaker, a tailor, a jeweller. In the past, this was all one great interweaving from soul to soul. It does not exist any more. Therefore our mental hospitals are overcrowded. These are things which are not understood today, but they are nevertheless a reality. We cannot any longer go back to a time when a tailor made perhaps twelve suits a year. The economy of today would not permit it—but we have to bring about this moral influence in other realms.

Comment. The world is hungry for what we could produce. People are not satisfied with all the artificial, mass products. Many people stop to look at the display in a Yugoslav shop near us; you can see that they are nourished even by simply looking at the hand-crafted things.

Comment. The number of that type of shop is growing every year.

Dr. König. It is understandable.

Comment. In this realm, probably more than any other of our cultural efforts, I feel that we stand on an equal level with the villagers. Our ideals are common ideals. The use of machines, for instance for sanding wooden blocks, is constantly balanced by work that is done by hand.

Comment. In South Africa a special situation exists in regard to adornment. The natives will prove to be our main market because they are a growing economic sector. Add to this that the natives by tradition and by nature produce a great amount of adornment; a tremendous variety. Nowadays however, factories are producing it, and thereby taking away this activity of the natives. We can perhaps help with this particular social problem by producing gradually for the native what he himself gives up.

Dr. König. Everywhere special problems will arise. I am convinced in America it will be particularly important to produce adornment, and under no circumstances to fall in with the mass-production trade.

Comment. In America they now copy Egyptian jewellery.

Comment. In America most jewellery is made by big machines in big factories, and everybody buys because it is cheap. Handcrafts have a hard time to exist.

Comment. During our talks and lectures I found confirmation for a feeling I have carried for some time. It is connected with the development we have spoken about—making things in our villages, also living a certain lifestyle in tune with the general development of the world, especially its technical development. Today there are huge machines, often worked by only one man. In walking through Botton Village I found old-fashioned tools, implements, bowls, troughs where the cattle were watered in olden times. Standing now in these times of modern technical development I ask myself: Where is the limit? Where can I say, as a human being having some insight and possibility of judgment, 'I have here a wooden bolt keeping a wooden door in its place; it is so perfectly made that beauty arises out of the form and out of the function so that this bolt cannot actually be replaced by a better, a more perfect one?' There are many other occasions when we have the opportunity to act with full consciousness against modern temptations and to say 'No' to the modern, mass-produced article which is neither beautiful nor practical, although we remind ourselves often enough not to ride a romantic or a 'folksy' horse. We ought to be far enough advanced to make choices and pick out here or there the value of things and work with them.

Dr. König. We have to accept tradition as far as it is justified, but we also have to recognise the boundaries. When we come from the spiritual world, we carry a certain amount of thought-life with us into this earthly life. Quite clearly we could not go on without it.

Similarly we must take real tradition with us, so that we can continue. The danger is in looking back—hankering after the past—and trying to bring all this into our present time.

Third Lecture

Karl König

Given on the morning of 1st February 1963

Dear Friends,

The three lectures of last year's conference introduced us to what will gradually form the background of our work in the villages. It was a threefold approach. In the first lecture we spoke about the general existence of the mask. In the second lecture we went on to approach the human soul in her reality, and we did this by means of Rudolf Steiner's picture 'Light and Shadow'. Finally, in the third lecture we approached the threefold human being by way of the threefold constitution of man and of woman. Something similar has taken place this year, in so far as in the first lecture we tried to look again at the mask. In doing so we established the threefoldness of the mask as mask, adornment and clothing. Then yesterday, when we spoke about the human soul, again something was revealed which can be called threefold, in so far as we began to realise that there is a breathing process in the human soul, an inbreathing and an outbreathing, similar to the breathing process in our physical existence, except that this breathing process goes beyond birth and goes beyond death. It implies, in Rudolf Steiner's words, the longing of the human soul: in exhaling to become world, in inhaling to become man, and to be man just at the crossing point between in- and exhaling.

The wholeness of the human soul revealed itself when we spoke about the 'midnight hour' between death and rebirth and the 'midday hour' between birth and death. The soul is thus engaged in a continual coming and going, reaching from yonder to here. Today we will again approach the threefold constitution of man and

119

woman, and try to take a further step with the help of certain indications which Rudolf Steiner has given. We have to more and more enliven within us this tremendous new image, the image of 'Threefold Man', which you will no doubt understand is one of the fundamental leading images which we have to carry within us. And if we do this by means of the constitutional appearances in man and woman, we will simply try to illustrate what lives as archetypal existence in every human being. Dear friends, this now gradually emerges as the threefold background of village life, in so far as the co-worker has to live together with his young friends. I would also add, and you will now understand what I mean, that it is the threefold background of the 'shepherd' existence, because the 'shepherd' has to know all that reveals itself in mask, adornment and clothing. Out of this revelation he has to reflect to the human soul the going back beyond birth into past lives and the going forward beyond death into future lives. Then we may look at the constitutional threefoldness of man and woman, and out of this draw possible conclusions for our inner existence. By doing so we again create leading images in our soul, in which others can reflect themselves.

I am certain that you remember very well how we tried to describe the differences in the three types of men and the three types of women respectively. You have studied this, some of you very thoroughly, and found many examples in past and present literature. All this has now come to life and has created clear leading images. I am grateful that you have done so, because in this way we will learn to speak the language of the constitution, which means we learn to speak the language of the threefold human being. It is, however, an entirely different thing from merely understanding this language. Usually we are satisfied when we understand certain indications which Rudolf Steiner gave, but that is not enough. It is even more important to proceed from understanding the language of these indications to the ability to speak this language. It is important that you understand what I mean because otherwise we will not live up at all to what I indicated. Our English friends are usually quite satisfied when they grasp one or two foreign words, but it would be much more satisfying for them if they were able to speak whole sentences because that would help them understand what it means to speak the language of constitution.

Let us go on and learn to speak the language of constitution. If I now use colours *(draws on blackboard)* it is not meant to express the woman, or the man, or any kind of judgement; it serves only to distinguish. You remember that the three constitutions in the woman give expression particularly to the senses, whereas in man it is the nerves and the central nervous system (the cerebrotonia). You remember all this. Then here in the woman it is the lungs, whereas in man (again, this implies no judgement) it is the heart. In woman it is the limbs, whereas in man it is the metabolism. And only the whole amounts to the real threefold existence. Can you follow what I mean? We could also see that here is thinking, feeling and willing *(see Illustration 14).*

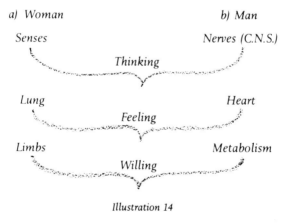

Illustration 14

But, (if we are to go into details), is it not very interesting dear friends, and very significant that the constitutional type of the woman reveals itself in the senses connected with the outer world; in the lungs by breathing and in the limbs by working? In man, on the other hand, it is the central nervous system, the heart beat—which is entirely concerned with the flow within the body—and the metabolism, which is also concerned, so to speak, with itself. Now instead of this rather intellectual exercise to draw up a kind of profit-and-loss account of these two types of human existence, we should rather try to draw pictures which change intellectual evaluations into imagination: to see the woman with her senses, breathing and limb organization, and to see the man with his central nervous system, metabolism and heart organization. If we look at ourselves, we can almost understand how, in regard to her soul, the female frequently appears very much bigger, greater, more overpowering than the male. You can almost see the female spider and the tiny little male spider which after mating is immediately eaten up. But you also find this in many other realms.[13] What does it show? It shows on the one hand that this *(see Illustration 15a)* is all turned towards the world, and that this *(see Illustration 15b)* is all turned towards man. Here we meet again what we saw at the 'midnight hour': we find the longing for the world (the exhaling) and the longing for man (the inhaling). May I remind you of the two quotations from a lecture by Rudolf Steiner which I mentioned to you last year. He said that the woman carries the wholeness of humanity in herself, but in such a way that she regards it as a gift from the whole of the cosmos. Man carries mankind within himself in such a way that he always regards it as a riddle which he is not able to solve or penetrate.[14]

In these two indications of Rudolf Steiner you find expressed in beautiful words what reveals itself here *(see Illustration 15)*: on the one hand the exhaling tendency of the soul of the woman (her senses, the limb organization and breathing); on the other hand the inhaling tendency of man towards the riddle of man. It is between these two that the soul expands her being.

Going a step further, can you begin to imagine how the rhythmic system of these two experiences itself? Torn outwards by her senses, torn outwards by her limbs into the outer world, the rhythmic system of the woman needs to keep together. Pressed inwards by his metabolism, pressed inwards by the nervous system, the rhythmic system of man needs to expand. So we learn to understand the expanding into activity of the male and the preserving tendency of the female, and thus we learn the different words of the language of the threefold human being. Given up to the world, through the senses and limbs, the woman needs the element of 'preserving'

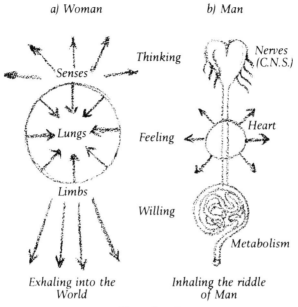

a) Woman   *b) Man*

Thinking — Nerves (C.N.S.)

Senses

Lungs — Feeling — Heart

Limbs

Willing — Metabolism

Exhaling into the World   *Inhaling the riddle of Man*

Illustration 15

(*bewahren*), otherwise she would be destroyed, dispersed into the world. Man would completely turn into himself were it not for the necessity of freeing himself from his own human nature, which makes him aggressive, necessarily aggressive. This, again, is an opportunity to understand human nature.

Taking another step, we now proceed into the realm of the human soul. Here we have the senses *(see Illustration 16a)* and here the central nervous system *(see Illustration 16b)*. So this is the side of the woman and this is the side of the man. The senses give us perception: we perceive the world. Here *(see Illustration 16b)*, on the other hand we form, out of the percepts, our concepts and ideas. Next comes the rhythmic organization: where we breathe, the lungs; where we have our pulse beat, the heart. And now we have to enter into physiology and into the higher rhythms of the human soul. Dear friends, what does our soul gain when we breathe? Why is the breathing, so to speak, the cradle of our soul life? We know, more or less, though as a stammering, first understanding, because time and again Rudolf Steiner has made it clear to us, that in the rhythmic organization the whole realm of our feeling is embedded and carried. But we can take a further step. We may ask: Very well, there is the breathing but there is also the heart-beat, so how does the world of feeling live between heart-beat and breath? Does our breathing carry within it one part of our feeling, and the heart-beat contain, as it were, something else? A certain degree of insight into our own existence will immediately reveal to us that in the breathing we have all that Rudolf Steiner describes as sympathy and antipathy. This is not the case with our heart; it has much more to do with our breath so that antipathy relates to inhaling and sympathy to exhaling. But what is left to our heart? Dear friends, it is something very special; something for which unfortunately only a German word exists, and this is the word *Gemüt*. It is usually translated as 'heart', which does not really cover it. You remember the lectures which Rudolf Steiner gave in Vienna in September 1923, *Anthroposophie und das menschliche Gemüt*, translated in English as *Anthropsophy and the Human Gemüt*[15] as there is no word in English sufficiently expressive of *Gemüt*. If we then ask what *Gemüt* is, we might translate it with the word 'mood', and 'mood' contains the element of *Gemüt*. But what is 'mood'? In German it is quite well expressed by the word *Stimmung*. And *Stimmen* in English means 'to tune'. You 'tune' an instrument. Thus the heart gives us the tune, which is the mood; it relates to our manifold moods, the moods underlying our life.

a) Woman		b) Man	
Senses		C.N.S.	
Perception	Thinking		Concepts/Ideas
Antipathy			
Breath	Feeling	Pulse-beat	
Sympathy			Gemüt/Mood
Limbs		Metabolism	
Doing	Willing		overcome
Forcing			deny
Yes			transform

Illustration 16

124

If you study the life of a great man, say the life of Goethe, whose daily moods you can follow from his diary, you will find, as Rudolf Steiner points out, that Goethe's moods were quite different before 1790 and after 1790. And if you ask what the year 1790 has to do with the moods of Goethe you will find that this is roughly the 'mid-day' of his life (1749–1832).

He lived for about forty-one years before and after this date, and before and after it the moods were different. Rudolf Steiner says that moods are determined, on the one hand, by everything we have experienced, and on the other hand, by all we are going to experience: all that has been and all which is to come meet here in the present. Both combine to give us the mood, the *undertone of life*. This mood is also an illustration of what I tried to describe yesterday as the 'mid-day' of life; it is experienced by the human heart. So these two sides *(see Illustration 16)* are different. This *(16b)* is more permanent—moods; this *(16a)* is more fluctuating—sympathies and antipathies.

Now let us take a further step and look at the limbs. On the male side we have metabolism. Again, dear friends, we know that here we have thinking, here we have feeling, and here we have willing. Do we understand this? Are we now able to distinguish, to illustrate, how the will works in the limbs and in the metabolism? Dear friends, who of you has asked himself what the distinction is between will in the limbs and will in the metabolism? What is it? I have the impression there is a very clear distinction; a distinction that we have only to recognize and we will understand it immediately. What is the nature of the will in our limbs? Which type of will do our limbs carry? Dear friends, in our limbs there is 'doing', forcing, outer activity; I could say, the 'Yes'. And what kind of activity unfolds as willing in our metabolism? It is something we know but we have not yet started to speak this language. When we eat we have to use our will to overcome, to transform, to deny what is given us from the world. Activity is turned inward, and so I write 'overcome'; I write 'deny'; I write 'transform'.

I am sorry it is so complicated, but you know the story Rudolf Steiner tells of the Spanish king who was not very bright and therefore said, 'If I had made the world it would have been much simpler'. I have to apologize that it is very complicated. But we have come some way. You see here *(Illustration 16)* the side of the male, and here the side of the female. We cannot say, however, that only woman has sympathy and antipathy, and only man has the *Gemüt*, or that only man has the power to overcome and say, 'No', and that only woman always says 'Yes'.

Now we have to learn how Rudolf Steiner describes the difference between man and woman. He explains that man has a female etheric body, and woman has a male etheric body, so that in man the physical body is male but the etheric body is female and in woman the physical body is female and the etheric body is male. Dear friends, I know that great difficulties will now arise, and I do not expect that you will be able to accept this great complexity in one go. But all will be written down, and gradually as you preoccupy yourself with it you will understand and then make it your own, so that you can speak this language.

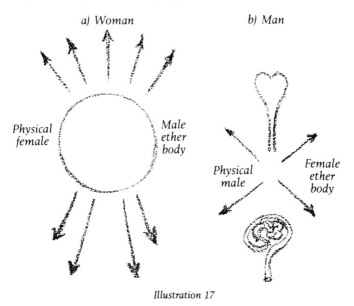

a) Woman *b) Man*

Physical female Male ether body

Physical male Female ether body

Illustration 17

I will now return again to the pictures, to the images *(see*

Illustration 17). On the one side we have the senses, the limbs, the rhythmic system; on the other side the central nervous system, the metabolic system, the rhythmic system. This *(see Illustration 17a)* is the woman, but it is woman in so far as she carries a male ether body, and this *(see Illustration 17b)* is man, in so far as he carries a female ether body. This is the physical female *(17a)* and this is the physical male *(17b)*. But you see, this *(17a)* is physical and etheric, and this *(17b)* is also physical and etheric. Then in man and woman it is crossed. You can see how the physical body of man forms the limbs, how it physically fashions the sensory organs, and how the physical body of man is physically turned to the world, while the physical body of the woman, formed in roundness, is concerned with herself. But now what is physically woman is in its etheric stucture male, and what is physically man is in its etheric structure female. It crosses over so that the male ether body unites with the female physical one; the female ether body unites with the male physical body.

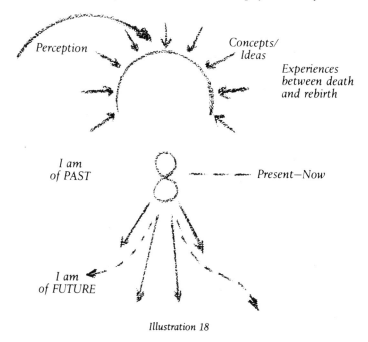

Illustration 18

Dear friends, this is a further step in understanding this most complicated form and existence of Man in thinking and feeling and willing. But we have not yet finished. Time and again when Rudolf Steiner speaks about threefold man he points to the human head organization, which he says is gradually on the way to decay. He even calls it a kind of regression. He says the high time of the head is past, and that now, step by step, it recedes, regresses.

We can understand this if, for instance, we observe how the hardening forces more and more take over in our head organization. Rudolf Steiner expressed it in the following way:

> The head organization of man is no longer involved in a progressive evolution, rather it is regressing. Man's head arrests ongoing development at a certain point and then actually regresses.[16]

To this I would like to add that not only are all the illusionary tendencies of the human head finished, but that exactly the same process also happens to the whole of our globe. The earth, too, has passed the peak of its development and now regresses. Our limbs, however, express something entirely different, and here Rudolf Steiner makes a very interesting observation. He says:

> Arms, hands, legs and feet (this organization also continues internally), this whole organization of the extremities is just the opposite of the head organization. It is an over-development, development beyond the normal measure. If one were to study evolution in relation to these conditions one would see that this development exceeds what Man needs between birth and death.[17]

Then Rudolf Steiner adds:

> Let us for the present look only at the exterior. There we see the organization of hands and arms in connection with the breasts, the secondary sexual organs; similarly the legs in connection with the primary sexual organs, which serve propagation. Thus the extremities are physically in connection with all that makes Man look physically beyond himself. In its very centre the limb organization serves not

only the individual human life but those elements which
reach beyond it, namely the soul-spiritual. The spirit-soul
basis of the extremities reaches beyond the requirements of
human life between birth and death.[18]

Rudolf Steiner confirms this when he points out the fact that our
head organization is formed out of the past, out of former lives. And,
dear friends, we have expressed often enough that in our head and in
our face we simply see nothing else but the result of our former life.
Therefore it is the end. It is—and you will understand me now if I use
the word—it is the mask of our former existence which we bring
with us.

But the limbs all point to our next life. We all know that out of the
activity of our limbs, out of the deeds that we do by means of our
limbs, we form the head organization of our next incarnation. Rudolf
Steiner describes it in the following way. He points to the fact—and
remember what we have just drawn—that through the head
organisation we have our perceptions, but we also form our concepts
and ideas. You can read this for yourself very beautifully described in
a lecture of 14th May 1918, where he says the following (and this is
very subtle, dear friends):

> If we would be able to remove all our sensory impressions and
> ask what remains, we would suddenly meet our own ego, but
> we would meet this ego as it was in our former life.[19]

So behind all sense experiences, behind all our percepts there stands
I myself as I once was in times past. And there is a continuous struggle
as Rudolf Steiner calls it, a continuous struggle between our sense-
perceptions and the ego of our former life—a struggle with the
concepts, with the ideas, with what we generally call 'thinking'. So I will
write here 'I am of the past' (see Illustration 18). Now our formation of
concepts and ideas rests, as it were, on a substrate, and this substrate
also stretches back; back to all the experiences which we had between
death and rebirth. So that when we think, in reality there lives in our
thinking what our experiences were when we prepared ourselves to
enter into this present earth existence. Rudolf Steiner says:

> Thus at the place where perceptions appear, there works the

previous incarnation and at the place where concepts appear there works the life we experienced between death and our present birth. The moment we develop powerful thoughts, we at once tap the resources of those experiences which we made during the time between death and rebirth. And what are these experiences? They are our ego. If we only develop thoughts which come to us from outside, which only appear in our soul because they are given us by outer circumstances, we invariably weaken what we have brought along from the time between death and rebirth. This, however, means that we weaken our ego.[20]

If we now turn in a similar way to our limb system, to the system of our will, and if we remember the distinction which we learned just half an hour ago between the 'yes' forces and the 'no' forces of our will, between the forcing and doing and the transforming and overcoming, then we are able to say on the one hand that in all we do, in all we force, we are already preparing the 'I am' of our next life, while on the other hand when we meet houses, meadows, towns, villages, men, or streets, these are all results of what we have done in our former life. The 'yes' forces of our will prepare the next incarnation, and the 'no' forces of our will prepare the life between this death which stands before us and the coming birth. This whole life is nothing else but an expansion of what here in the will of our metabolism we try to overcome, to transform.

During life on earth we overcome and transform the substances of the world: after death we overcome and transform all the karma, all the senses, all the deeds, good and bad, which we have committed. Our metabolism, in so far as it is will, is a preparation for the life between death and rebirth. Our work, the results of our actions, is a preparation for what is to come in our next life. And in the centre there stands the twofold attitude of preserving and acting. The male and the female part, in sympathy and antipathy and also in the mood, represent the 'now', the 'present', between birth and death on earth.

Now you will understand if I say in conclusion that it is only man and woman together who are able, in community, to prepare the safety, the security, of the egos of those who live with us, be they villagers or children or we ourselves. This is because it is the woman, with her male etheric structure, who is turned towards the world, who creates the space of what we term 'security', and it is the male, with his female etheric structure, who prepares the space of man in himself, the space of 'certainty'. Between the security which the woman creates, and the certainty which the man brings about, the safety of our children, the safety of our young friends, is assured. So it is not one of us alone, but we together, in as far as we are male and female, who create the 'shepherd' existence of our villagers. If we could look back into the past, into our former lives which have led to this one, and if we could visualise this, or if by magic we could suddenly make it apparent, what would we meet? You will now understand that we would meet masks—the masks in all their possibilities and variations. Therefore I said ours is the mask of our previous existence. Therefore the masks appear bizarre, tragic, horrible, evil, animal-like. All that has once been now faces man in the form of the mask. What is going to be is shrouded in the darkness of the future, and we cover it with our clothing. We veil those parts which lead into the future. Therefore we do not cover our face but expose it as our mask; but we veil the rest of our existence in order to cover (and now understand what I mean) our limbs. Only the limbs are naked, nothing else. The limbs, with the accessory organs, do appear naked because we are not only afraid, we are also ashamed of the future. It must not yet be shown, so we veil it. And here, where we are now between birth and death, (and we have, as Dr. Kolisko said, 'the time of our life'), we try to make the best of it so therefore here we use adornment to reassure ourselves in our existence on earth; to try to be and to become what we are.

So these things begin to merge, to flow together, and thus help us understand one another. I think you will agree that now certain leading images have again started to rise in us, and this is our task.

Discussions with Dr. König

Question. I followed the first part of your lecture until the point where physical and etheric became crossed. Would it be possible to go over this once more?

Dr. König. It means such a tremendous mental effort on your part; it would be a pity to let you forego this. It is so important to make the effort in order to learn to speak this language.

Comment. I suddenly had the impression that the types which you drew last year do not hold good any more, because then you pointed out that the outer appearance (the constitution) and the behaviour go together. Now, I think, this doesn't hold good any more.

Dr. König. Beautiful eyes are the expression of the etheric and not of the physical. Let us say you have beautiful eyes—and there is no doubt that everyone of you has beautiful eyes, because as human beings we have beautiful eyes. This is the expression of the life of the ether, of the shine of the ego, of the strength of the astral as they manifest in the physical body. If you start to go to sleep but have acquired the ability to keep your eyes open, your eyes are no longer beautiful. And you can pretend to be awake as much as you like, but anyone can tell immediately that you are not. You see, what I want to avoid is the creation of one-sidedness: to say that the woman is so and so. If you read books on men and women, the most opposing statements are made by people who really have great powers of observation. I remember a book, written some thirty years ago, in which the writer pointed out that the main characteristic of women is devotion—and proved it with hundreds of examples. Afterwards I read another book in which the most outstanding quality of women is described as anger and wrath. And you see both are perfectly right;

the one and the other. It depends whether you are considering the female physical body or the male etheric body. The male etheric—and now be careful—the male etheric in the woman makes the three constitutional types appear, because in their constitution the women reveal their male etheric body. In their constitution the males reveal their female etheric body. For physical and etheric male are alike; physical and etheric female are alike: and then it crosses over. Can you understand?

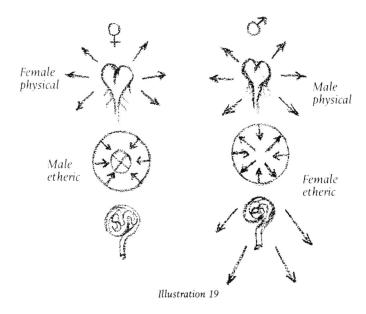

Illustration 19

I shall take quite different colours in order to make it clear. I will now draw the woman—not the female etheric, not the female physical, but the woman: a woman. And to make it quite clear I will use red for the physical and orange for the etheric. And I draw the woman and then I draw the man. The physical body of the woman—and I stay within the pictures which I have now made. Can you understand? And the etheric body of the woman. And now I draw the physical body of the man. For this is man, as he has a physical body. You see each form has two substances—a physical and an

133

etheric. And this is now the constitutional type of man: because it is the female ether body. Female etheric (I write it down), male etheric. Female physical, male physical.

Comment. I believe the difficulty one has with the thought that the etheric works upon the thinking is because we are still inclined to think in terms of chromosomes. . . But perhaps we can think of what you described as breathing between day and night. . . The male creates the female physical.

Dr. König. In occultism you hear the following sentence: the male is the karma of the female, and the female is the karma of the male. You cannot deduce that the woman becomes the man, etc. The female and the male in other ways have their karma together. And you see that the male etheric wants to become the opposite in the next life, and vice versa. As a male I have, so to speak, the karma of the female which I am going to be in my next life (if I say 'I', please don't take it personally). But our next life's karma in the opposite sex, that is what we carry in our ether body. This is generally known in occultism, when it is said the woman has the karma of the man, because the woman in this life is going to be a man in the next and vice versa. But, dear friends, to imagine the male etheric structure in the woman and the female etheric structure in the man—and in addition to find the soul and psychic qualities which relate to it— enables us more and more to understand the difference between the two sexes. You see, physically man is the power and the will which enforces, which says 'yes'. But in the background, in the more subtle sphere of his existence, there is the tendency to overcome, to change as the woman usually does in her will. And the woman in her subtle existence calls forth, enforces, inspires and so on. We should attempt to follow this up with a great degree of earnestness and fashion it more and more into images—even if they are not quite right it doesn't matter, because the spiritual world makes very straight images out of crooked ones. Rudolf Steiner always gave a very straightforward indication to the speakers and lecturers. He said it doesn't matter at all if you sometimes make wrong statements because they are corrected by the spirit. This should not be an excuse for proclaiming a lie, but if by inner earnest activity some mistakes are made we need not mind.

Question. How do you think we should proceed if we now have co-worker meetings in our various places?

Dr. König. First of all you should continue with and finish last year's attempt—and only after you have learned to speak the language of last year should you start to take up the next. Before you have learned to play the previous scores, it will be difficult without proper finger exercises to play this one. Therefore if I were you I would not worry. You will already continually renew the work. Draw on this source—and then start to introduce one or another of the new things. It would be fatal if you said 'Last year gone—now this one.' If you have got far enough next year that you can start on this year's score it will be alright. These are things which cannot be forced. I can see you continuing with the basis given by last year's three lectures. If you don't know the fundamentals of addition and substraction, you cannot move on to multiplication and division.

Question. You said that behind the sense experiences lives the ego of the last incarnation, and we meet it in what we see around us. If one meets a person and knows him or her a little bit better, one feels that in this person there are certain features of his character which are very fitting to this incarnation—but sometimes it changes suddenly and there are features which do not fit in at all, and one then has the impresion one meets quite another person. If one can say that what we meet through our senses is the ego from the last incarnation—I wonder if there is any corresponding feature in the character of the person?

Dr. König. I think what we meet as astounding qualities, which cannot be blended with what we know of the person, does not go back to the past but belongs to the future; the future incarnation already throws its light, as it were, into this one. This is what we meet, because the meeting with the ego behind the senses is only possible for us ourselves—not with regard to another person. If we cut off all our sense experiences, which gradually happens when we go to sleep, then we meet the ego.

Editor's Footnote: *The following excerpts from Dr. König's essay, Hunde und Katzen—Begleiter des Menschen (Dogs and Cats—Companions of Man), may help to further elucidate the problem presented in the foregoing lecture.*

The contradiction can be resolved when we take note of indications given by Rudolf Steiner with regard to the two sexes. In a lecture on *Man and Woman in the Light of Spiritual Science* (Munich, 18th March 1908) he describes how round the turn of the century mutually exclusive characterizations of the sexes were being expounded. Some found the basic character of women to be wrathful;* another describes her dominant trait as devotion. Again '...another natural scientist concludes that the basic temperament of woman is best expressed as resignation, surrender or aquiescence; another describes it as lust for power; yet another speaks of her conservative sense while still another calls her the truly revolutionizing element in the world.'

Rudolf Steiner accepts all these contradictory elements and shows that their existence is justified as soon as we learn to see through the polarities. He first points to the fourfold human existence, which carries hidden within the physical body the etheric or formative forces body, then the soul organization and the ego. He says:

To begin with we are here concerned with the physical and etheric bodies. And already here we find hidden the solution to the riddle with regard to the relationship of the sexes. The being of Man is a peculiar organism, in so far as the etheric body is only partially a kind of replica of the physical body. With regard to sexual differentiation, the matter is otherwise: with the male sex the etheric body is female, with the female sex it is male. To begin with this may appear strange but in depth observation will soon guide us to an appreciation of this extraordinay fact: the hidden nature of every human being harbours some part of the opposite sex—the woman's deeper soul shows male traits; the man's shows female ones. When therefore man by dint of his exterior corporality becomes a warrior since this outer courage is tied to the outer organization of his body, then the woman is endowed with inner courage with the possibility of sacrifice and devotion.

---

* The German word 'zornmütig' has the sense of righteous wrath.

Learning and Working — The Karma of Vocation.

Third Conference
Held in the Camphill Hall, Murtle Estate, Aberdeen, Scotland.
18th–20th January 1964

First Lecture

Karl König

Given on the morning of 18th January 1964

Dear Friends,

The three lectures which are now to come will take a different direction from those of our previous two conferences of last year and the year before. To begin with, I would like to refer to these last two conferences, in order to let you know what I had in mind when we were preparing a basis for our work in the villages. You remember how, two years ago in January 1962, we began to describe the mask? We tried to understand that it is not the individuality we meet when confronting our young villagers nor, in fact, when meeting other human beings generally, but that during life on earth, between birth and death, every one of us carries a kind of mask which conceals his individual existence. In some people these masks are fixed from morning to evening, while in others the masks change from morning to evening. One could say, more or less, that those who are able to change their masks as often as necessary are more adjusted to the needs of life than those who continually bear the stress or the joy of their permanently fixed mask. Then last year we followed up the problem of the mask, we as it were enhanced it, we embellished it, and we came to learn that in addition to the mask there exists what, using a German word, we called *Schmuck*, adornment. And perhaps adornment in all its variety, is also a kind of mask, as is everything that we wear as dress, clothing and so on.

So more and more we learned to understand mask, adornment, and clothing as the three, let us say, determinants, the three constraints, the three masks of the individual in the widest sense of the word. We pointed out the history and development of masks, adornment and clothing, and in this way we began to gain a certain understanding of the way man lives here on earth.

Dear friends, to acquire an attitude of wonder—wonder at a mask, a piece of adornment or clothing, when we see the differences all over the world and how different people dress—to wonder about this educates the innermost part of our soul. So we should meet our villagers not with judgment but with wonder. During our two previous meetings I tried time and again to point this out. Let us learn to wonder and let us learn to accept—not to judge, but to accept. This was the one aspect. We then tried, within the realm of the mask, to describe the male and the female constitutional types according to the threefold nature of man. I don't need to repeat it: you have tried to work on this very extensively, and have formed a proper and (I hope) a fundamental insight as to who is a cerebrotonic and so on. But last year we also spoke about the three basic qualities of the soul, thinking, feeling and willing, in connection with this threefold being of man, who represents himself in the three different types of constitution. The moment we spoke about this, dear friends, we did not remain within the boundaries of birth and death, but we stepped across the threshold of birth, and across the threshold of death. We then tried to trace how thinking and feeling unfold in yonder world. We accompanied the three qualities of the human soul beyond the threshold of death, saw them separating one from the other, saw thinking and the power of sense-perception taking an entirely different path from the power of willing, and saw feeling follow an entirely different course in the world in which we live between death and re-birth. We came to an understanding of mask, adornment and clothing from a different point of view as we followed the path of thinking, feeling and willing across the threshold. We followed this path to the midnight hour. Thinking, in outbreathing, having become world now again strives to become man. We saw how the elements which lead the soul into the new incarnation are gradually collected and ordered. Further, we learned to appreciate, with the help of one of Rudolf Steiner's lectures, how the limbs are totally different from the head organisation.

You remember that we were compelled to describe the limbs as over-developed, whereas we saw the instrument of our thoughts regressing, starting to shrink (to use an image). On the one hand there is something which is too far developed; the instruments of our will, the limbs, and on the other hand there is something which is regressing, is already on the downward path: the head organisation. Dear friends, at this moment may I advise you not to forget this but to take it as a kind of exercise in order to train yourselves in your work when meeting our friends the villagers. Then you will not only see that the head organisation is round, formed by the all-embracing powers of the cosmos, and that the limbs are formed in such a way that centrifugal forces pour out through them from the centre to the periphery and from the periphery to the centre, but in meditating the Gestalt of head and limbs, you may let the head slightly shrink, direct it towards mummification, whereas you may let the limbs 'sprout', 'shoot', and overgrow their own form and existence. When you are able to carry these two images (the shrinking head and the sprouting limbs) you will understand the form, the mask of man, and how he stands in life; but at the same time you will understand how these two forms point beyond birth and beyond death. The head shrinks for the simple reason that it is the end: we bring our head organisation with us through the gate of birth. Between birth and death it dies. Our limbs, on the other hand, are born during the time when we develop within the womb and they increasingly develop, sprout, overgrow. They are, as it were, the promise which we take with us through the gate of death. At this moment, dear friends, we know for certain, without any doubt, that our life stretches not only from birth to death, but that there is another part which complements it. Our existence is not bounded by these two gates but we are a whole, a complete circle, which comes and goes from birth to death and from death to re-birth. The one without the other is like a flower which is severed from its root, from its soil, and has in point of fact no reality whatsoever; it is an artificial product. This is the first thing we have to contemplate: life between birth and death is completed only by the life between death and re-birth. We know this but it has to be brought alive within us again and again.

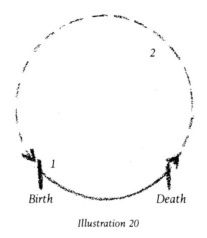

Illustration 20

Dear friends, this part (1) is the one which we usually consider; but this part (2) has to be added if we are to do justice not only to our villagers but to ourselves and to all men on earth. However, this is not everything, because there is a third aspect: reincarnation (3). You must understand that in these two (1 and 2) reincarnation is *not* included. It is the circle of life. When Nietzsche had his evil intuition, whereby he suddenly thought he had discovered the key to all existence, the eternal wheel of coming and going, he remained within this circle. So unless we add (3) we entirely forego the Christian aspect of reincarnation. We must learn to understand, dear friends, that an individual is developing, unfolding, learning, working, enhancing, 'becoming' within this *wheel* of coming and going. This is a first introduction, and I would be very grateful if you would keep this vital aspect in mind as the basis for all our further deliberations.

Let us return to the head and the limbs; to the gate of birth and the gate of death. Let us understand (looking back to last year's lectures) how the human soul has the two fundamental qualities of thinking and willing. Thinking is connected with the head and the brain organisation, and willing is connected with the limb organisation. I apologise if I keep repeating this (I may be boring those who have made a complete study of this matter), but I can't

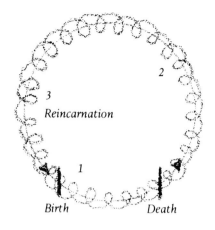

Illustration 21

help it; I have to put some fundamentals before you. Our thinking, dear friends, does not take place in isolation. You will remember how Rudolf Steiner describes the sensory-nerve organisation in which the nerve organisation is the physical foundation of our thinking, and in which the sensory organisation is the basis for all sense-perception. In the sphere of the head both are intimately connected. So we have thinking and sense-perception. Now, if willing has its polar correspondence in thinking, what then corresponds to sense-perception in the sphere of the metabolic-limb system? In the same sense as Rudolf Steiner describes the system of senses and nerves do we have a system of metabolism and limbs. And here nerve corresponds to the metabolism and the senses correspond to the limbs. This, too, would be good for contemplation, dear friends, because it is usually all thrown into the same pot. Willing has its physical foundation in our metabolism; we eat and digest, we transform substances, and these substances are lifted up into the different organs where they are re-created, and become our own carbohydrates and proteins. This gives us the physical foundation for our willing. But strictly speaking willing does not live in our limbs. General willing, as soon as it takes hold of our limbs, is transformed into what we might call doing—to do, or to make.

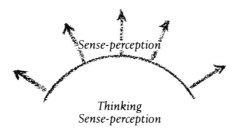

Thinking
Sense-perception

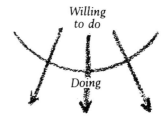

Illustration 22

And now please understand: on the one hand, sense-perception out of which arises our thinking; on the other hand, willing out of which arises our doing. And out of this doing, dear friends, work develops, and work which is ordered, and which has a certain specialisation, develops into occupation. So profession, or calling, belongs in this sphere; the sphere of our limbs in which the transformation of our willing takes place. No doubt it is connected with food; you must eat otherwise you can't work. There's no alternative because you must give to your *will* a physical basis which derives from metabolism. And now you will realise something—at least I hope you realise it, dear friends. Sense-perception leads to thinking which leads to willing and becomes doing; and here in between stands the human being. All this (our thinking) comes from the gate of birth. All this (our willing) meets us from the gate of death; it goes through the gate of death.

Dear friends, let us repeat. Willing turns into doing; doing turns into work, ordered and specialized labour becomes occupation. If I go to work and for several hours I perform a skilled job (which means a specialized kind of labour), I have ordered my willing; I have ordered my will in such a way that gradually my head can become disengaged and my whole existence is in the sphere of will. This is the past *(see Illustration 23, left)*: this is the future *(Illustration 23, right)*.

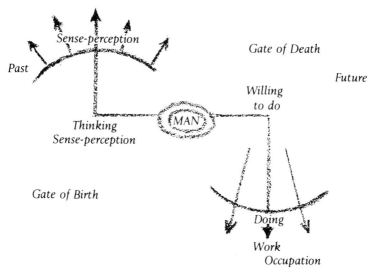

Illustration 23

And now we come to a very great question. Dear friends, have you ever asked yourselves what the polar opposite of work and labour is? What do you think? What is the polar opposite of working?
Question. Leisure?
Dr. König. No, leisure is nothing. It's an illusion; in point of fact it doesn't exist.
Question. Does it have to do with the midnight hour on yonder side?
Dr. König. No.
Question. Does it have to do with something here on earth?
Dr. König. Of course, of course. What is the opposite of work?
Question. Sleep?

Dr. König. No.

Question. Play?

Dr. König. No, because even in play there is a fair amount of work. You know how tired you get when you play.

Question. Contemplation?

Dr. König. Yes, yes?

Question. Thinking?

Dr. König. We are getting a bit warmer, but not yet hot at all.

Question. Ordered thinking?

Dr. König. That's a bit warmer still. Can't you coin a word which expresses all this?

Question. Meditation?

Dr. König. No. It is something we all have to do here on earth, without which we can't live. Dear friends, I am not putting riddles before you.

Question. Eating?

Dr. König. No!

Question. Learning?

Dr. König. *Yes!*

On the one hand we have the whole world of learning, and on the other hand the whole world of doing. I'm sorry I asked you instead of telling you but now you won't forget it. We have to learn, but we have to learn throughout that time when we hardly do any work, namely in childhood, in youth. That is the time when we learn. We begin by accumulating a certain amount of knowledge, and this kind of accumulated knowledge which is imparted to us becomes more and more ingrained in us. It makes all the difference whether one goes to school, say, on the continent of Europe or here in England or in America, (although today it is no longer so differentiated), because the kind of knowledge, the way of learning, and the art of teaching (if it still is an art) are so different that the results can hardly be compared. But it is all learning. We learn in many different ways, (and we will discuss this later), but as we learn we are being formed. We learn to remember, we learn to suffer, we learn to think, we learn to forget, we learn to know; and by knowing, by forgetting and remembering, by suffering and enjoying, we are increasingly formed out. The world around us works on us. I am afraid this is a little difficult. When we learn, something outside us works on us: the teacher, the priest, the doctor, the parents—all those people and friends who are around us when we grow up. They form us by words and sometimes also by deeds, and we learn. Sometimes we don't want to learn, but mostly we have to. Learning gradually forms us so that we can turn to working. But when we work (and now you will understand) something else faces us in the same way that as children we were faced by those who taught us: we are confronted by the substances of the earth. We plough the field, we weave, we transform substance—glass, metal, iron and so on—and through our work, the earth and its substances, plants, animals and minerals, are *educated*. Can you understand what I mean? They now have to suffer, to remember, to be formed, to become, in the same way as we had to learn when we were children. The priest, the teacher, and in a way also the doctor, are the representatives of the powers of the world, and the powers of the world educate and transform the child, the growing person, so that he in turn can transform, become man or woman, and teach the earth. This is a process, dear friends, which recurs innumerable billions of times throughout the ages. It is the true process of becoming, of developing, the true process of the evolution of mankind.

LEARNING
Priest
Teacher
Doctor --------------------------- *Workman*
Artist
Thinker
WORKING

Illustration 24

Here *(Illustration 24, left)* stand the priest, the teacher and the doctor as representatives of the powers of the world. Here *(Illustration 24, right)* stands man, who learns in order to work; man who becomes a labourer, a craftsman, a worker in all manner of specialized occupations; who also becomes an artist in every conceivable form of art, and also a thinker—because in the thinker, in the philosopher, the will engages itself in what Rudolf Steiner calls the 'movement of thinking'. These are the six fundamental types of occupation. But the workman, the artist and thinker do not represent the powers of the world. They represent the powers of man. The powers of man teach the earth. The powers of the world teach man. In this way learning and doing are the great tools for every kind and type of man.

This again can show you how *learning* comes from the gate of birth, is carried over from the past, so to speak, and how *doing* goes into the future through the gate of death, and thereby prepares the future. Thus Man is placed between past and future; and in this image you learn to understand what I previously called the third element which is added to the individual's path through the circle of life between birth and death, and death and re-birth.

Now every one of you has thoroughly studied these lectures, *The Karma of Vocation*,[21] at least I hope so. You will remember, dear friends, how in the third lecture Rudolf Steiner refers to Jacob Boehme, and how he described him as the great mystical philosopher who was also a shoemaker. Then he says something very strange (but very understandable now, after what I have tried to tell you), that the mystical philosophy of Jacob Boehme is the end, and that shoemaking is a beginning. In making the soles of the shoes for the good people of Görlitz, which was the town that he lived in, Jacob Boehme prepared the future of this earth. So one could say the seed of shoemaking was much more important than the whole beautiful and wonderful mystical philosophy of this man. The development of our earth, dear friends, proceeded from ancient Saturn, to Sun, Moon and to our present Earth; these are the four incarnations of our earth so far.

The earth (for those who like to be more informed, I will write it down) is here and will further develop into Jupiter, Venus and Vulcan. On Saturn what was warmth developed more and more and is now the foundation of all that, as will, lies behind our potential to work here on earth, for instance when we mend shoes. This work then develops further and further, and will be Vulcan at the end of all days. In that lecture Rudolf Steiner explains how on Saturn everything was in deep sleep. On Sun and Moon it gradually woke up and only became clear day-consciousness here on earth. Something

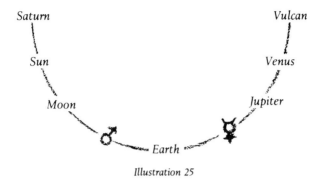

Saturn

Vulcan

Sun

Venus

Moon

Jupiter

Earth

Illustration 25

similar begins again here on earth. We produce in a state of deep sleep. We make a nail, for instance, or hundreds of thousands of nails and these nails are made in a consciousness of sleep. They are severed from us, they go their own ways, as do not only nails but everything we produce. These ways have a task for the future, because what we have put into the work of making nails as sleep-consciousness will gradually become a dream, will start to wake up, and become conscious at the end of all time, on Vulcan.

Dear friends, this is the meaning–I would also say it is the mythology–of labour and occupation. It is a first step in our understanding. There is still a great deal more I should say, but thus far we have come. I want to close now but we should continue to talk about it after a short break.

Discussions with Dr. König

Question. Rudolf Steiner gives the indication which you mentioned. On the other hand you spoke of the thinker, whom you placed in the sphere of the workman, and I wonder whether you could explain this a little more?

Dr. König. I said the thinker in so far as he uses the mobility of thoughts. In doing so even some of the thinkers of the present time belong to the work sphere. There are not many, in fact there are very few, for it has nothing to do with the intellectual aspect of thinking. But the thinker belongs to this group to the extent that he plants ideas into men, out of which their working abilities and capacities are enhanced. I didn't say 'philosopher'; Jacob Boehme was also one, but his philosophy was so replete that it became fruit and did not remain seed. He developed a complete concept of the world, as did Swedenborg too. The seedlings of thinking are something entirely different. Rudolf Steiner's *Philosophy of Spiritual Activity*[22] is seedling thinking. It does not give a complete image of the world, which would be a philosophy. Schopenhauer did that. He developed a philosophy. Kant didn't. Kant investigated the act of thinking, the act of willing, the act of doing; this is thinking.

Question. When you spoke about waking up, through the development from Saturn, Sun, Moon and so on, I understand that it was our consciousness that woke up. Now when nails are produced in the sleep-consciousness of the will, what exactly happens?

Dr. König. You see, this leads us to very difficult images. In making nails, you create beings, elemental beings, and it is the development of these elemental beings which brings about a gradual unfolding of culture. It's not so much the nail that matters, but the making of it. The joy when you make a nail, or pour wax to produce a candle, is not the important thing; the process of pouring itself produces beinghood. This then develops through further stages.

Question. Do these things also happen, and do they have the same results, when our feeling, our joy and our thinking are involved in the act of work?

Dr. König. Yes, don't worry, they should be involved, but the value for the future is a different one. It would be quite wrong to go to work with a long face and work in order that elemental beings develop. They develop anyway; they develop by the process of working. You can't keep your work continually in your consciousness. It's quite impossible. But joy or sorrow or boredom or whatever, will develop in your consciousness. This belongs to the past. For the present it is the doing that counts; the continuous shifting of the shuttle or treading of the wheel, or whatever it is. That is the important thing, because out of it the form grows, the earth is educated, the substance shaped. Beings sprout and develop into the future. This is the process.

Question. What happens when a machine runs quite by itself, when there is no person consciously involved?

Dr. König. Different types of beings develop, of course. We will always have to face this; we can't help it. It's necessary, because also in the elemental world the battle, the fight between good and evil has to go on. We also shouldn't worry about this, but we should know it.

Question. How does one look at work which has no visible product, such as the shopkeeper's work, for instance? If you take the shopkeeper, he doesn't make anything. And what about people who have to guide others, who don't create a nail, but who somehow help in their being created? How does that fit in?

Dr. König. All this is the result of the past. You see, the *priest*, the *doctor* and the *teacher* in one life stand for the past. The *workman*, the *artist*, the *creative thinker*, on the other hand, stand for the future. This is necessary. Perhaps in the next life I will not be a doctor and a teacher, but can be a humble workman, and then I will do something for the future. At the moment I only represent the past. And why not? I mean you would have ordered the world differently, I know. But nothing will come out of the future if you don't have the past, so you can't turn your back on the past. How can you prepare the future without the past? Is it not wonderful how things fit together? But we shouldn't think that the doctor and the teacher are the most important people nor, especially, the priest. It is not a question of better or worse; they represent something which is the one side of the scale of life, and it is only both together, with the fulcrum* in between, that represents the fullness of existence. You would be very surprised if I asked you who stands at the fulcrum.

Question. To return to the preceding question, to the person who doesn't work but guides. Is this not connected with the idea becoming ideal? Rudolf Steiner says every idea which does not become an ideal, kills.[23]

Dr. König. It is the transition from the past into the future. Therefore I said there are two forms of thinking: philosophy and seedling thinking. The seedling which is idea becomes ideal. The 'ideal' is the fruit. If you read Leibnitz's philosophy, for instance, it's a wonderful fruit but it's so big that you can't bite into it—quite impossible—you can't eat it.

Question. Can one say that in so far as the doctor, the priest and the teacher do not guide or transform will into labour they are only the past. . . ?

Dr. König. I said they *represent* the past, but they bring about the future in man. Dear friends, this is not meant as a scale; they should

---

* Dr. König used the Greek word *hypomochleon*. The modern word 'fulcrum' is being used throughout the text.

stand next to each other. Also the other three, the workman, artist and thinker, should stand next to each other. And now the great question, who holds the balance? What would you think?

Question. The merchant?

Dr. König. No, he does something.

Question. The shepherd?

Dr. König. The shepherd is also working, although he is only walking. He is watching and sitting, all of which is a great strain. But there are some people who really do nothing; I mean they do no work. There are actually two.

Question. The banker?

Dr. König. No, that is working, he does a lot. No, then you could also include every office worker and so on.

Question. I meant in the sense of handling a lot of capital.

Dr. König. Yes, there is a connection. You can definitely say that on this line there stands the banker, and a little bit further along stands the merchant. But here at the fulcrum we have the sphere of rights; and here stand people. They are the soldier and the judge. Of course, soldiers have to fight only at times but they put, as it were, their love into existence; at least in former times it was the case that by their position they ensured a certain stability or instability of existence. And here also belongs the occupation of being a mother. One shouldn't forget that.

Priest		*Soldier*		*Workman*
Teacher — *(Banker)* —	*MOTHER*	— *(Merchant)* —	*Artist*
Doctor		*Judge*		*Thinker*

Illustration 26

153

Question. Considering the course of an individual life one may say that in childhood one is on the side of learning and in adulthood more on the side of working, but what is it that makes one turn around? What is it in the life of an individual, or also in the life of a whole age-group, that brings about the change, makes one turn around in this way?

Dr. König. What would you think? This is a very interesting and important question?

Question. Doesn't it go even further; that the next step is to become a teacher, to step back into the other sphere?

Dr. König. What do you mean?

Question. There is the side of the priest and the doctor and the teacher, from which man learns, and he takes what he has learned and then it becomes doing. As teacher or doctor would he then not belong to the other side, the work sphere?

Dr. König. Yes, but I don't think we should mix things up. The child develops, in the way in which I have indicated, through learning. And behind him stand the three who guard him. And they are here *(left side of Illustration 26)*. Of course we are all engaged in both learning and doing; therefore we always have a little bit of a priest, doctor and teacher, and a workman, artist and thinker in us. But here in our diagram we have separated the occupations from their roots. I mean we are a teacher in our soul. But if we *become* a teacher we develop that faculty, and all other five, six or seven faculties remain dormant. We should really become woolly if we were to say we are everything; of course *potentially* we are everything. But now we have at last developed this view of a separation so let us keep it.

Comment. I think that the karma of vocation plays into this question. In our development we reach the point where we must decide what profession or vocation we wish to follow.

Dr. König. Exactly, exactly, only this doesn't answer the question of how we come to this transition *(from the left to the right side of Illustration 26)*. Because karma works here as well as there. But how is the turning-point to be found?

Question. Is it not at the end of puberty?

Dr. König. Yes, you can say it is during the time between puberty and adulthood that this turning point occurs. But the question is: *How* does it occur? and *Why* does it occur?

Question. You spoke at the beginning about the gate of birth and the gate of death. This turning point seems to me also like a gate, like the eye of a needle, because it brings about a complete change. But I wonder what this gate is?

Dr. König. That's the thing. There is definitely the seven-year period between puberty and adulthood. If, dear friends, you are interested in this vital question I would like to say the following. Let us ask ourselves what it is that our children (I now mean the handicapped ones) and our adult friends (our villagers) have in common besides their handicap. Let us ask: Why is it necessary for them to be segregated from the general stream of life, in childhood as well as in adulthood? I gave a lot of thought to this question and I have come to understand something which is a first step, and which will have to be developed further. Let us first describe the adult person. In those in whom we see the handicap as a generalized symptom, we find that out of themselves none of them, or hardly any of them, are able to build the platform on which they can stand in life. One can use such expressions as 'they lack adaptability' or 'they don't fit into their environment'. This is only a description. The reality is that if left to themselves, if left alone, they are unable to find the karma of their vocation, to find the type of work, to hold the work, to which they are assigned by karma; and even when they have learned to do this they are unable to create around themselves an environment which is their own. Together with others, especially when helped, they can do it. You see what I am after. This is the reason for creating villages, for creating workshops, farms and so on—to bring to them something which they are unable to find and to forge for themselves. This is the one thing.

With the children who are in our care it is the same in the sphere of learning. They are, in point of fact, not able to learn unless they are specially taught *how* to learn. This is the great art of curative education—to teach our children *how* to learn. We must persevere in this. We must mould, we must guide them in such a way that the act of learning is increasingly made possible for them. Can you understand what I mean? The handicapped person has to be taught *how* to learn; then he can learn. It is our unskilled way, in not teaching them *how* to learn, that prevents them from learning. And for the others, the adults, it is the inability to create their own basis of existence in life. If you build them a workshop, put them in it, see that they work and choose their work; it's all right. Can you understand that this is in line with your question? It's not the full answer, but I am trying first of all to sort the whole thing out.

Question. Isn't it true that very many so-called normal young people don't any longer know which direction to take?

Dr. König. Yes, but at the moment we are not including the modern type of youngsters in our discussion, who we know are also in need of special care. There are also thousands of children today who are not any longer able to learn unless they are taught *how* to. This point of view relates to our present time, but it is not to a general point of view that I am trying to draw your attention. I know this, and we are agreed on it. But the essential thing is that the handicapped person lacks the ability to lead his own life; to order it in such a way that the environment becomes his own and that as a child, in the process of learning, he is not yet able to learn. Can you follow this, dear friends? You see, these are very difficult problems, as soon as one begins to think about them. We take them for granted. And I would advise you, when you speak to other people, that you always make it clear to them that this is the reason why we create villages. The handicapped would not be able to create villages for themselves, but they can sustain them and, by sustaining them, they will increasingly be able to insert their own existence and create their own environment. This is the task: that it should not be our but *their* environment which *they* create.

Question. In our time the world of work and the world of learning are partly extremes, are caricatures. Is this because the balance is completely lost?

Dr. König. You see, the banker and the psychologist increasingly assume the judge's position, and the merchant increasingly assumes the soldier's. But I don't want to go into the special problems of our time before we have understood the fundamentals. Let us go a step further with the following question. Let us ask what we need in order to be able to learn? I mean, what do we need as faculties in ourselves; which faculties make it possible for us to learn? A large part of modern psychology is occupied with finding out what capacities are needed in order to learn. Not thousands but hundreds of thousands of experiments, most idiotic ones, are made to discover how white mice or grey rats learn which way to go in the maze, when to stop, and so on. But in truth what kind of powers, or faculties of our soul, create the process of learning? I ask the question again, dear friends, in order to help you not to forget it. With what faculties do we learn?

Question. Memory?

Dr. König. Memory is one of the main things, but there are more distinct faculties.

Question. Instincts?

Dr. König. Animals learn through instincts.

Question. Inbred instincts?

Dr. König. Yes, out of these we are made. But which one helps us to learn? Which inbred instinct makes it possible for us to learn? What does the little child do?

Question. Imitate?

Dr. König. Imitate! You see, this is the first step. Imitating means repeating. Repeating means memorising. Memorising gradually leads to memory and learning. And where does imitation come from? Where does it have its root? To imitate is not an instinct, it is one of the fundamental powers of our soul. It lives in our soul. It is a characteristic of the soul to imitate: you could also say of the astral body. It imitates, and imitating gives rise to repeating which in turn gives rise to memorising, and with memorising, powers of memory are awakened. And the powers of memory create the capacity to learn.

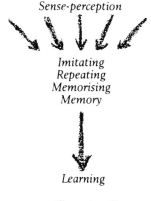

Illustration 27

You see, dear friends, when the little child goes to school, it learns in a general sense. It begins to understand authority, and the ordinary (in this sense we can say 'normal') child begins to use these powers. The process of learning is naturally accomplished through imitating, and it is this that many of our handicapped children cannot any longer do, especially those who are mentally deranged, psychotic. Therefore, repeating becomes locked in itself, memorising goes its own way, and learning no longer occurs unless we put our curative efforts into one of these spheres to make learning possible. That's the one thing. And now we start working and we ask the same question: What makes work possible? In the sphere of learning we pointed to sense-perception which brings this about. But working?

Question. The will?

Dr. König. Certainly—but we know this already. Here is the side of the will *(right hand side of Illustration 26)*. But which powers of the will, which grades of the will, which spheres of the will are necessary in order that a workman even gets up in the morning—not to mention our villagers? With the word 'interest' we touch something. But at once I would have to ask what is interest?

Question. Of course there is necessity?

Dr. König. Necessity? Yes, if you understand it rightly. But very few understand it. It is not the necessity expressed in the wage-packet.

Question. The need?

Dr. König. That is another whip, yes. It's quite right, as far as it goes.

Comment. I've been thinking of the origin of work, according to the Old Testament. Work did not arise until after man had been cast out of Paradise, where he did not work. I would say that therefore this was the necessity. It was laid upon him to work by the sweat of his brow.

Dr. König. Exactly, exactly. He also didn't need to learn before the fall. With eating from the Tree of Knowledge he had to learn. And thereby the need to work arose. You see again how these two hold the balance. Yet I still have to ask which inner faculties we had to develop in order to be able to work. There is the pressing need, but what makes this need rise up in us so that we go to work?

Question. I mean one thinks of the realm of love or compassion?

Dr. König. No, no, you wouldn't get further with that. No, I'm afraid not.

Question. Hunger?

Dr. König. Hunger? Well, it is also an outer need; we can cover it with 'need'. But how can I work? I wouldn't go to work when I'm hungry; I would rather die than work.

Question. Sympathy for creating?

Dr. König. Yes, yes!

Question. Self-expression?

Dr. König. Self-expression, yes, though it is more or less the same.

Question. To have a certain idea of work, what one wants to achieve?

Dr. König. You wouldn't find very many people who have this ideal to achieve something. They are glad when they do something; they enjoy themselves. But what you called self-expression, that is a very important thing.

Question. Enthusiasm?

Dr. König. That also belongs to the word self-expression. You can do this in many different ways.

Question. Is it a kind of responsibility one has inside?

Dr. König. Yes, yes — what is this responsibility which one has inside?

Question. Conscience?

Question. It must have something to do with conscience and responsibility—with the connection between the soul and the body. It is a certain way of self-expression that the body is used in accordance with the soul's intent.

Question. Is it not the will to transform the earth?

Dr. König. In the children who come up from Hades, that wish is there—but in no others.

Question. Establishing oneself on earth?

Dr. König. Which is again the same as self-expression. This is all in one direction, dear friends. Self-expression, responsibility, conscience. But what do you have to do in order to work?

Comment. I only want to explain an experience. If one is in the realm of learning for any length of time, one feels the strong urge to *do*, in order to be able to live. I experience that one has lost one's roots if one is in the realm of learning for too long. We work in order to establish ourselves again, and this in turn is an enhancement for learning.

Dr. König. Oh, definitely! I mean it's quite clear that time and again these two have to be brought into balance, otherwise you are out of gear.

Question. Is it not connected with sympathy—or, sympathy for creating?

Dr. König. Yes, as I said, but it is no more connected with sympathy than learning is with antipathy. You must hold off, you must distance yourself from something in order to understand it, and you must be a little sympathetic to the substance which you mould—otherwise you would not do it.

Comment. A child's work is play, and play is an organized activity, an activity which is simply innate in all of us, and work is a higher organized activity.

Dr. König. This I think is the step which we need. I wouldn't call it 'organized', I would call it 'ordered'. It is a certain amount of ordering which you have to bring to your activity, to your doing. As soon as you realise this you can trace work back to ordered activity; and then look for the root, for the fountainhead, and find it in conscience, so that behind this ordered activity we have responsibility (or whatever you like to call it), and conscience. And now you see how memory and conscience are as it were the two sides which guide learning and working. This is very interesting. One could still say a few more things, but it would cloud the issue. Let us take this with us now, and start tomorrow with the question which is still unanswered: What is the fulcrum, the centre point, where memory turns into conscience? Where is and what is this fulcrum on which, so to speak, the scale of memory and conscience rests? Agreed? Thank you very much.

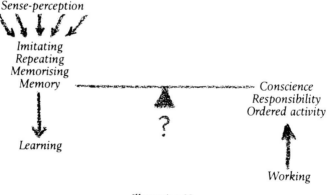

Illustration 28

Second Lecture

Karl König

Given on the morning of 19th January 1964

Dear Friends,

Yesterday morning we concluded our session with a question which pointed to a most important problem: Where, when and how does this fulcrum occur in the life of almost every human being between birth and death; this turning point when the period of learning is transformed into the period of working? What is it in the lives of every one of us that brings about, in one way or another, the replacement of learning by work? Here, dear friends, we turn to the central point of our whole discussion. We have to ask ourselves where and in which way does this special turning-point occur? It means not only a metamorphosis of certain powers into others, but it is almost a kind of changing over of one thing into another. In this lecture I will try, step by step, to make this point clear. The answer is a difficult one. It is not so easy to say 'here it is'. But if you study Rudolf Steiner's lectures entitled *The Karma of Vocation* you will find that in certain places he refers to the actual turning-point, without directly calling our attention to it.

Let us recall again what we achieved in yesterday's session. We unfolded, as it were, the image of human life in such a way that we spoke of *learning* and of *working*, and in between (see last diagram of previous lecture) we placed the fulcrum to which we have referred, a fulcrum which occupies the space between memory and conscience. We said that the platform, the basis, of learning is memory; the fountainhead of work is conscience. Out of *conscience*, through *will* and *ordered labour*, *work* arises. Learning is grounded in imitation and repetition. Repetition is also necessary when we order our work. Repetition is necessary to strengthen our memory. Repetition is, in fact, a necessary servant of everything we have to achieve in life. And those human beings who are unwilling or unable to be repetitive when necessary, those who think 'I know it anyway' or 'I can do it anyway', and therefore must quickly embark on something new, they will forego one of the most important tasks for man here on earth; the task of shouldering the cross which each one of us must bear. If one remains, metaphorically, a young horse, jumping about from place to place, from work to work, from deed to deed, from thought to thought, then one will miss what is in fact the task of man on earth: to learn by repetition, to work by repetition, and to bear the bridle of our karma. There is nothing we can escape: if we don't face our karma in this life, it will be much worse in the next one. This by way of introduction! After each chapter of this lecture you will get a kind of spanking, dear friends!

Let us again pose the question: What is this fulcrum? Before being able to find the answer we must turn once more to the archetypal image of man going from one life into the next. I've shown this to you yesterday and you can read it time and again in Rudolf Steiner's lectures, especially in the ones which preceded[24] those on *The Karma of Vocation*. There he indicates a most important key to human karmic existence; that the human head in one incarnation is the result of the preceding incarnation. Our heads, here and now, are the result of our former life, which is the consequence of our karma.

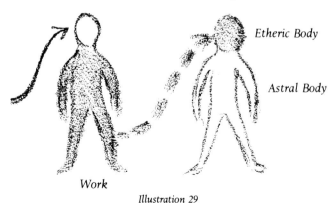

Etheric Body

Astral Body

Work

Illustration 29

We acquire our limbs and body in this life, first in the womb of our mother, and then gradually in living, learning and working, and these then, in going through the gate of death and expanding throughout the life between death and rebirth, form out our head in the coming incarnation. In this next incarnation a new limb-body system will be acquired, which will again go on to form the head organisation of the subsequent life. Dear friends, we should never forget this image, and we should gradually learn to see it in everyone we meet, not knowingly but as a kind of basic experience: 'I see your head, and it speaks to me as if I were able to decipher the letters of your former life. I meet your limbs and your body, and they assure me of your existence in the coming life.' And each head and face, dear friends, should be experienced like a question mark leading back into the previous life in which the limbs were formed out, the work was done, life was suffered and experienced, and in which emotions grew and feelings were present. All these things, through the metamorphosis between death and rebirth, find expression in the head. I asked you yesterday to make it one of your daily meditations to see the head as a kind of regressing, shrinking organism. It is old; it is the end, and in our present life it is dying and will never be renewed. The limbs, however, are sprouting. They are working, and all our intentions, impulses, wishes, good and evil deeds, lead forward vigorously in order to form a new head organisation in our next life.

As soon as we grasp this we will understand that the work which we do, whether as joiner or goldsmith, as weaver or husbandman, as shepherd or officer—whatever work we do in this life—is carried over into the next life and will form out our future head organisation. And if we were able to read the 'letters' of our head and our brain organisation, of our face and our eyes, of our chin and the way we speak, we could almost experience what kind of work we did in our former life. We should understand this, dear friends, and we should increasingly make this a fundamental experience when we meet our children and young people. The head organisation is of course also instrumental in bringing about individual motor-activity, constitution and so on, and so all of this is to a great extent (not completely, but to a great extent) the result of what we have done in our former life. Please make this alive in yourselves as vividly as possible. If in your former life you were very rich (I don't know whether any one of us was), and had no need to work but only to eat, imagine what the head would look like. One can almost imagine it. But if from poverty it was necessary for you to work hard, perhaps even to go hungry, then naturally your head and face organisation would look quite different. Many distortions in certain types of children (brain injuries, malformations) are the result of unfulfilled deeds in former lives, and will be the result of unfulfilled or distorted deeds in their present life. Thus one life is integrated into the past life and into the future one. The work we do now forms our head for the next incarnation, decides our constitution, and builds up our motor organisation.

We must now ask ourselves how this is done, dear friends. Let us turn to the fifth lecture of the cycle *The Karma of Vocation* in which Rudolf Steiner describes man as an instrument, a musical instrument, with four strings: physical body, etheric body, astral body and ego. He then presents the image of the various sources of karma playing on these strings, and thereby different melodies arise. Speaking about the karma of vocation in a previous life he says the following:

> We have to do with a whole complex of forces which project themselves from one incarnation into another. Now we must consider what relationship exists between this complex of forces and the human being in so far as his life flows along between birth and death. Here he or she is really an instrument with four strings, played upon by this complex of karmic forces. The four strings are the physical body, ether body, astral body, and the ego. Karma plays upon these. According to the measure in which the one or the other—the ether body, the astral body, or the ether body together with the astral body, the physical body together with the astral body, the physical body together with the ego—is swept by the bow of karma (if we may be permitted this comparison with a violin, which also has four strings) the individual human life comes into existence. The tones of these four strings of human life may play into one another in

the most manifold way. For this reason it is very difficult if we wish to speak, not in mere empty abstractions, but in concrete detail, to decipher the individual life-melodies of man, since it is possible to decipher them only when one is able to see how the violin bow of karma plays upon the four strings of a human being.[25]

He then continues:

It will be found that something appears in a more definite way in the developing human being which we may call, in a sense, the inner peculiarities consolidated, as it were, through the corporeality, by the whole character of its demeanour—but only in so far as this demeanour comes to expression in the posture of the corporeal being, in the gesticulation of the corporeal being, in the whole carriage of the life. I refer to what is there taking solid form—not all, to be sure, but a great part of that which causes a human being to be thick-set and short, to have a shorter or a longer figure, which causes him to walk in a certain way, with a firm tread or with a dancing gait, to mention radical contrasts—in short, whatever has to do with the corporeal part of the carriage in life. When we observe this—not all but a great part, as I have said, of what thus appears in the developing human being— this is derived from karma: the effect of the vocation of the preceding incarnation.[26]

This clearly supports what I described today. I would say that to a great extent the individuality is expressed in movement; the way a human being walks, the kind of steps he makes, and the way he presents himself, is the result of the vocation of his former life. Rudolf Steiner now asks the very important question: On which side of this four-stringed instrument does the karma of vocation play, in order to bring this about? It is very important that each one of you understands this question. The answer is given by Rudolf Steiner in the following way:

The astral body then works back upon what had previously been developed. If one knows this fact, if it has been derived from spiritual-science, it can then be observed also on the physical plane. The astral body works back in such a way that it transforms, in accordance with other karmic forces, what had resulted during the period from the seventh to the fourteenth year out of the purely vocational karma. In other words, two antagonistic forces struggle with one another here in the human being. One group of forces gives him form; these come more from the ether body. The other body of forces works against these, and in part paralyzes them; so that the human being is compelled by these other forces, coming more from the astral body, to transform what has been forced upon him by the vocational karma of his previous incarnation. In other words, we may say that the ether body works in a formative way. For what is manifested as the bearing in the physical body, as one's carriage, is derived from the ether body. The astral body works in a transforming way. Through the play of the two forces, which are really in a bitter conflict with one another, much comes to expression having to do with the working of the vocational karma.[27]

In these sentences, dear friends, we meet the central point of our discussions. It is the etheric body which has the formative power for all that I have just described: the individuality of our movements, the way we present ourselves, our constitution, whether we have short or long legs—whether we are one or other of the types described in the lectures of last year and two years ago. It is the etheric body which forms this. Rudolf Steiner then explains how the astral body works against this and tries to form it in a different way, or to reform it. And through the interplay of these two powers (actually a fight, a real battle, between the two) a great deal of the working of the karma of vocation is expressed.

Dear friends, if we learn to understand that the ether body carries, as it were, the impact of the karma of vocation, and that the astral body tries to work against it, that these two fight each other, then we approach an understanding of what we called the fulcrum. But how does it come about? We know that our etheric body is born when we are seven years old. This etheric body, (the personal one, not the part which is given to us by heredity), this etheric body which we carry with us develops our personality, between the seventh and fourteenth year, out of our past existence. Then at puberty our astral body is born and this astral body, wanting to fashion its present existence and to pave the way for the future, stands against the etheric body. These two begin to fight. This is the battle of puberty. This is what we see when our young boys and girls suddenly or gradually either succumb to the strain of this battle or fight through it and then slowly become themselves.

But this now works together with other karmic currents; for we must also consider the physical body. With reference to the physical body, what comes primarily into consideration during the first period of life is the question how the human being has placed himself in the world by means of his karma. Even the kind of physical body we have depends upon this; for we place ourselves, by reason of our karma, in a certain family, which belongs to a specific nation. For this reason we receive a very definitely formed body. But this fact, that we receive a definitely formed body, is not the main thing, for just think how much is dependent upon the course of our life, upon the situation into which we have entered by placing ourselves in a definite family. Through this very fact, the point of departure is given for a vast amount in our life. And, as a matter of fact, during the time in which the physical body is especially developing, during the first seven years, there are active in the physical body—or we had better say around the physical body—forces derived in this case not from the vocation and all that was related to our vocation in the previous incarnation, but from the manner in which we have lived in previous incarnations associated with other human beings, while we stood in this or that relationship during that preceding incarnation with this or that other person, not in any particular part of our life—this belongs to another field—but throughout the entire life-time. This is now worked over. We bear this with us through the portal of death; and by reason of these forces, we bring it about that we place ourselves again in a certain particular family, in a certain particular situation in life, so that we may say that what actually places our physical body here, in a sense, and works through our physical body, also determines our life situation. This continues to work further, of course, through the following lives, and this meets its counterbalancing force through the ego. The ego works in a dissolving way upon life-situations; but it works in conflict with what is already determined in the life-situation. We may, therefore, say: Physical body—creative of the life-situation; ego—transformative of the life-situation. Through the united action of these two in this struggle, another current of karma takes hold upon life. For there are always present in a human being both that which tends to keep him in a particular situation and that which tends to remove him from this particular situation.

1. Physical body: creative of the life-situation
2. Ether body: formative
3. Astral body: transformative
4. Ego: transformative of the life-situation

That is to say, 1 and 4 work in a primitive manner upon one another and 2 and 3 upon one another; but these strings work also, in turn, in the most manifold other ways with one another. The manner in which we enter into relationship during one life, according to our karma, with new human beings depends upon 1 and 4 in their connection with one another. But this is to be traced back, in turn to our life-relationships in earlier lives. The manner in which we find our life-relationships in the matter of our daily work, our vocation, is connected with 2 and 3 and their reciprocal action one upon the other.[28]*

But in order to take a further step we must learn to understand

---

* The editor feels that this quotation from the same cycle, which was not included in the original lecture, throws further light on the matter.

something more. (I told you it would be difficult, but I know you don't mind.) Dear friends, man is born into this world in such a way (whether male or female) that he brings with him a nervous system, especially a brain, which is more or less a plain and un-inscribed millionfold tablet. It is empty; it has certain structures, certain features, but it is not individually, personally inscribed. It carries, as it were, the horoscope of our birth but not much more. Only when the baby begins to breathe, to move its limbs and its head, to sit, to utter the first vowels and consonants, to stand, to use fingers and hands, and to imitate speech; only then do each one of these mobilities, each one of these experiences, all these millionfold perceptions and images which are seen, heard, felt; only then do they inscribe themselves into the brain and thereby make the brain a servant of the individual. What is achieved by this, especially during the first three years, when we learn to stand and walk, to speak, to think and to understand? Each one of these processes moulds, forms and inscribes our brain, thereby making it the organ of learning. Without these three years it would be quite impossible for us to create the organ of learning. Please begin to understand that each one of us has a personal and individual organ of learning.

Dear friends, our brains are different according to our mother-tongue. An English brain is different from an Austrian; an Austrian brain is different from a Norwegian, and therefore the process of learning is different. We can't possibly escape the habits of language, the habits of gesture, or the habits of habits. The language of the people wherein we are born, the gestures of the tribes into which we come, be it in village or in town, are different. In Aberdeen you move differently from how you do in London. A Londoner would never toss his head each time he said 'Good morning. How do you do?', or 'What is the weather like?' In London it wouldn't be understood. In Greece people nod in order to say 'No'; we shake our heads. This is inscribed in each child, and we carry it with us. It prepares our model of learning. And naturally each one of us has a somewhat different view of the world, because the tablets are differently shaped, and they therefore mirror differently the innumerable things which are given to us from birth onward. If one person is different from another, he or she need not be impossible; they are simply *different*. They must be different, dear friends, because their learning is shaped differently, due to the differences of the instrument which is prepared during the first three years and later throughout the years up to seven, eight, nine, ten, eleven. It is most important, dear friends, that we understand how we bring the karma of vocation, the whole karma of our last life, with us. It works and forms the head and brain, and from it our constitution derives, by means of the ether body which forms it. Short or long, strong or lame, whatever it is; whether a muscular man, a pycnic or a leptosome, and so on.

But another stream works into this, namely the stream of our mobility, of our mother-tongue, of everything we experience by means of the senses, by imitation and repetition, and through the special games we play as a child. By all this our memory is built up. Then when we go to school, how we learn to write is inscribed into our brain; how we learn to read is inscribed into our brain; how we learn mathematics is inscribed into our brain. The brain is formed by our motor-activity, by our learning, by our language. But, dear friends, it is only formed up to a certain point in time, that is until the moment when the astral body is born and begins to fight against what we have brought with us from former lives. Time and again I have to point out that although we have centres in our brain for our verbal activity, for writing, for reading, and centres for understanding, nevertheless the brain of a joiner, of a goldsmith, of a blacksmith or a potter does not have a centre for joiner's work, a centre for turning the wheel, or a centre for hammering: such a centre does not exist.

Why is this? Why is it, for instance, that we have no centre for driving a car, although we drive a car more often, perhaps, than we write? Why do we have no centre for climbing or for going downstairs and such things, yet we have centres for reading, writing, speaking and moving? All that we have learned up to ten, eleven or twelve years of age is still inscribed into our brain; a brain which is moulded according to the work we have done in our former life. But as soon as our astral body is born and begins to stir within us, it starts to come into its own and fight the result of the previous existence in our ether body, and at this moment something very special happens.

I will draw your attention to this now for the first time. You see, our brain is an instrument for the word, but it is not in any way an instrument for the work. The word, in so far as it is expressed in speaking, writing, reading or even in moving, finds its inscription in the tablet of the brain, but as soon as we begin to work the brain rejects. The brain does not any longer *want* what we do to be inscribed into it. Literally, dear friends, the brain shows an aversion, and this aversion is turned into something very special. At the moment that the astrality of man is born, when the brain does not want to accept inscriptions by the motor-activities of work any more, at this moment, out of the fight between etheric and astral body, an organ comes into existence which one could almost call a 'phantom'. This phantom is the image which we have of ourself. You see, it is during puberty, sometimes a little bit before and sometimes later, that the phantom of our ego-image comes into existence. The brain rejects, but we go on moving. And in the mobility and the fight between astral body and etheric body, in the rejecting powers of the brain which are almost, yet not quite, physical—and therefore we cannot see but can experience them—in these the phantom of our ego-imagery is created. As soon as I say this you will understand what I mean, because each one of us carries an image of himself (or herself) in him or her. It would not be very kind to speak about the images which we have of ourselves because these images are usually rather above the average. They must be! We *have* to imagine, in our ego-phantom, that we are V.I.P.'s, Very Important People! There is no alternative. But, dear friends, the longer a young person is given the opportunity to learn, the more pliable, the larger, the better this ego-image will be worked out. On the other hand the quicker, the sooner a young person is driven from learning into working, the harder, narrower, stronger, this ego-image is made. This ego-image, dear friends, is with us throughout our life. In the same way as we have an inner image of our bodily structure, so we carry with us an image of ourselves. But it is not our true self: it is the personal, the individual phantom-image of our self; an image which is so different that its powers are not *radiating* ones, but are *drawing*, inhaling powers. Therefore inevitably, in one way or another, we have to relate whatever we read, whatever we see, whatever we experience to ourselves. In some way or other we must establish a connection between a person (usually the great guy in a film) and ourselves. We identify with the hero in a novel, and whatever he does has meaning with regard to ourselves.

This is absolutely necessary, dear friends, yet it is just like a figurehead carried in front of us. If I call it the monogram of our individuality you will probably understand what I mean. And we can now ask more exactly: How does it work? How does it form itself out? Dear friends, I will express it in an image. The helmet of our etheric body, our astral body and our ego is mirrored in the physical form of our head organisation, and within this, here in the forehead, appears the figure-head, the monogram, of ourself. This monogram is continually renewed by the work which we do and is continually kept alive in its form by all that we learn. Learning and working build our ego-image. But, dear friends, it is this ego-image which stands in front of spiritual knowledge in every one of us: it bars our way to spiritual knowledge. It is this image of ourselves, whether we are high or low people, whether we are good or bad, whether we are a genius or a poor wretch, that stands in front of us and prevents us from accepting that there is a world of the spirit. Here, in the forehead, is the mask of the monogram which makes us say: 'I am a great guy, and nothing else matters to me! I'm not interested in what will come later.' Because it has been built up over five thousand years of the Kali Yuga and is now here, it is *ingrained*, it is *inserted*, and it causes man to cut off the arm *(see Illustration 30)* which brings learning with him through the gate of birth, as soon as he goes through puberty and becomes himself.

Learning   *Working*

Illustration 30

We all have this arm of learning severed when we go through puberty. Then we begin to work. We become men, carrying the monogram on our forehead, and thinking we know who we are. But it is the phantom of our ego. Our astral body tries to help us over it, but it is filled with egoism. Our ether body carries the forms of the past life, yet we can speak, we can think, we can write, we can read. But the monogram is there. And through acceleration in the development of our children, as a result of the insidious system of our schools and universities, we encourage or allow a more and more radical severing of this arm of learning so that the last image of a spiritual world is wiped out, and we become nothing but a number in a mass society. Radio, television, newspapers, magazines, all make this monogram in each one of us as similar as possible, so that the heroes and the heroines we adore are always the same. And we forget, dear friends, that since the fifteenth century something else has started to develop in our forebrain through the work of the Archangel Gabriel. This is a new organ* which, if we use it, will gradually enable us to make the monogram of our ego-phantom transparent, as we gradually learn the laws of metamorphosis in plants and animals; the work of the etheric and astral body; the form of head and limbs. Living Goetheanism will be the key to open this organ and to lead us into the world of the spirit. This kind of learning is one of the main tasks which will have to establish itself in your villages. Although the Christian services are of the utmost importance, they still leave the human being enshrined between birth and death and here bless him with the wonderful powers of the sacrament. But today something else must be added when he works, and this is the beginning of an insight into the work of the spirit, so that man himself creates anew this arm which the world has cut off when he went through puberty; the arm of learning which reaches up to the spirit.

We need to understand this more and more, dear friends, because this is the central point of the question with which we will have to deal tonight: how to make the step from school to village in such a way that schoolboys and girls become villagers. Because especially in the boys and girls, the youngsters, the young people with whom we have to deal, the handicapped ones, the psychotic ones, the deranged ones; in them the monogram of the ego-image is either too great, too small, either not established at all or diffused, not fully worked out. Or it is even the case that from time to time one monogram changes into another. At one moment the ego-image can forget its reality and put up something entirely different which then again is replaced by the original one. We will have to learn to understand this monogrammatic

---

* This is referred to more fully in the quotation read after the lecture.

sign in the other, and also in ourselves. It will be of the greatest importance that we learn to judge objectively what our ego-image looks like, for instance in the way that we react. Only when we do this, step by step, will we become objective towards ourselves; neither rushing into decisions nor fearing to decide, over-reacting, being offended, creating vanity in ourselves, or striving for power. All this, dear friends, is intimately connected with the ego-image, which is, as it were, an intermediary organ for the time between 3101BC and AD1899. We still have to carry this sign of the Kali Yuga with us, but it will come to an end. And what we meet in our young people, the so-called normal ones, is the gradual, very slow disappearance of the ego-image. They don't care any more, but therefore they lose strength, interest and everything that makes social life possible at all. And the strength, the suffering and the disruption which is to come in the next decades (not centuries, dear friends, but decades) will be such that we can hardly imagine it, neither you nor I. But it is bound to come. And this is what we have to try not to ward off but to fill with new possibilities, at least in little seedlings like village communities, to which not hundreds but thousands will be able to hold on.

If you look at the statue of the Representative of Mankind, at the way Rudolf Steiner has imagined it and formed it, you will see the gesture of the Representative of Mankind with the upraised left arm and the downturned right hand creating the space in which man in freedom may again acquire learning of the spirit and undertake work for the earth's future. In this way we might understand the karma of vocation from a special point of view. Please learn to see, dear friends, that this fulcrum is the very peculiar but very important monogram of the ego-phantom which we carry in us, but which we have to overcome by the power of the new organ to which I referred.

We will stop at this point and tomorrow begin a new chapter that will conclude our deliberations.

176

Dear friends, the wish has been voiced that we have no discussion. We can't vote by raising hands, but I would propose the following and I hope you will agree. I was prepared to read to you certain parts of the lecture by Rudolf Steiner in which he refers to the new organ in our forebrain. May I do so, and then we can finish if there are no further questions? In this way Rudolf Steiner's voice will be heard, which is much better. I will read from the cycle *The Occult Significance of the Bhagavad Gita*,[29] the fifth lecture given on 1st June 1913. There he refers especially to this new organ. There are also other lectures in which he refers to it, but this, I think, is the most important one.

In this lecture he speaks about the introduction and the beginning of the modern scientific age, and then he says:

> Just as the epoch of natural science was prepared by Bruno's work in breaking through the limits of space, so will the firmament of *time* be broken through in the age now beginning. Mankind, imagining life to be enclosed between birth and death, or conception and death, will learn that these are only boundaries set by the human soul itself. Just as in earlier times men had themselves set as the boundary of their senses a blue sphere above them, and then of a sudden their vision expanded into the infinite spheres of space, so will the boundaries of time be broken through, those of birth and death. Set free of these there will lie before man's gaze in the infinite sea of time all the changes in the kernel of man's being as he follows it through its repeated incarnations. Thus a new age is beginning, the age of spiritual thought.
>
> Now if we can recognise the occult basis of these transitions from one age to another, where shall we see the cause of this change in human thought? It is not anything that philosophy or external physiology or anatomy can find of their own accord. Yet it is true that forces that have entered the active souls of men and are being used today to gather spiritual knowledge--these same forces, during the last four centuries, have been working at man's organism as constructive forces. Throughout the period from Copernicus to the

177

last third of the nineteenth century mysterious forces work in his nervous system during sleep. These forces were building up a definite structure in certain parts of the brain. The brains of Western people are different from what they were five centuries ago. What is under man's skull today does not have the same appearance as it had then, for a delicate organ has been formed which was not there before. Even though this cannot be proved externally, it is true. Under the human forehead a delicate organ has developed, and the forces building it have now fulfilled their task. In the coming cycle of history we are now approaching it will become evident in more and more people. Now that it is there, the forces that build it are liberated. With these very forces Western humanity will be gaining spiritual knowledge.[30]

Rudolf Steiner also explains that it is the Archangel Gabriel who was, as it were, the power behind these forces, building up this organ. So we could say that from the time of Paracelsus and Copernicus all this has been going on. And of course, if we don't take up these powers and forces in order to gain spiritual knowledge, like any other organ which is not used, it will simply fall gradually into decay, into the same decay into which mankind will also fall. Rudolf Steiner says it in these words:

We may give a name to these forces—for what are names? We can call them *the forces of Gabriel*. But the point is to gain a moment's insight into the supersensible where we perceive a spiritual Being working from those worlds into the human organism. A sum of forces, in fact, directed by a Being, Gabriel, of the hierarchy of the Archangels. From the fifteenth to the last third of the nineteenth century the Gabriel force was at work on man's organism, and because of this the power to understand the spiritual slept for a while. It was this sleep of spiritual understanding that brought forth the great triumphs of natural science. Now this force is awakened. The spiritual has done its work; the Gabriel forces have been liberated. We can now use them, for they have become forces of the soul.[31]

Third Lecture

Karl König

Given on the morning of 20th January 1964

Dear Friends,

The two lectures, of yesterday and the day before, covered more or less everything that I wanted to bring to you. In pointing to the figure of the Representative of Man, and in uniting the image of the statue with this very important relationship of the polar opposition of learning and working, the archtetypal image of the life of man here on earth is presented. It is presented from the special point of view of our work in the villages. Time and again it will be necessary that we take up and unite ourselves with this archetypal picture (the *Urbild*), and try to regulate our social life in the villages accordingly, so that step by step this seed will start to radiate strength and order into the surroundings. But I don't mean only the immediate physical and earthly surroundings, say the villages around one of our establishments. Such a seed will begin to work increasingly as a homoeopathic remedy into the whole social order of our present time.

Dear friends, you know as well as I do that Rudolf Steiner's attempts to bring the Threefold Commonwealth to life in the years between 1919 and 1925 failed entirely. During his lifetime the impulse was rejected, in spite of the many seeds which he had sown in the hearts and minds of tens of thousands of people. It would be futile to argue why it happened like that. No doubt the people who were then at his side were the least suited as helpers to establish such a thing, for they had no idea whatsoever of the social structure. They were quite unable to communicate with the workmen because they were bourgeois people of the best (and therefore the worst) possible kind. They were intellectuals who tried, with every good will but complete inability, to bring a social movement into being. So Rudolf Steiner stood more or less alone against two very formidable powers. The one formidable power was the Church of his time—churches of every possible denomination—and the other, equally formidable power was Trades Unionism in every guise— Socialist, Republican, Democratic, or whatever. These two powers, dear friends, are still alive.

But we, at this moment, are able to appear in a different guise and we do not need to proclaim it. We appear in the mantle of the task of caring for the handicapped, of caring for the land, of doing social work. In this way we are nevertheless able, though not as Rudolf Steiner imagined, to sow tiny little seeds here and there in as many places as possible. But we must remain in the background, because otherwise we would call up these two formidable powers, and meanwhile we must learn how to meet them. Please forgive me for speaking so bluntly, but the time is at hand when at certain moments such words are necessary. The village impulse, if we might call it that, is a new form in which to practice the idea of the Threefold Commonwealth. I do not imply in any way, dear friends, that our work for handicapped people is a means to the end of establishing the Threefold Commonwealth. Our work for handi-capped people is as earnest and as serious, as filled with the will and the enthusiasm to help, as it could be; but it has gradually revealed itself to be one of probably several possibilities to make the Threefold Commonwealth a reality. So whenever you are in despair turn to the ideas of the Threefold Commonwealth, and know that this is another opportunity, is another call, to try to instil into mankind the only available help for the social rejuvenation of our existence. I repeat, the *only* available help! I have already said, two mornings ago, that we will gain nothing but self-satisfaction if we shut our eyes to the present condition of life around us. It is not that we are better—perhaps in many ways we are worse!—but what we meet around us today is nothing but decay—decay of human conditions, decay of social conditions, decay which will only lead to rot and death.

Now if we take up such an idea as learning and working, and

permeate it with the image of the statue of the Representative of Mankind, knowing that this image is, as it were, inspired by the image of the Son of Man, then we have something which is worth living for, working for and fighting for. What I would like to do this morning, dear friends, is simply to explore one or another direction with you in order to discover the possibilities which this image can give us, so that you may learn, may understand how to use it. But I don't want only to show you that it is possible, for instance, to use it in such a way that you put before yourself, or before those with whom you are working, the great question of the two evils with which man has to battle and fight—the two evils which Rudolf Steiner has described in so many different ways, and whose names for us are Lucifer and Ahriman. If you take this image earnestly, you will immediately discover that it is Lucifer who is directly, intimately, connected with the whole sphere of learning. Look at this image and you can see it. He is the one who tries to hold us in the realm of the Spirit and not let us come down and tread the earthly ground, whereas Ahriman is connected with the sphere of working, and wants to make us shut our eyes to that which is above us and entirely submerge ourselves in substance, in matter. The one—Lucifer—is the Tempter; the other—Ahriman—is Evil, and between the Tempter and Evil we stand as Man. If you say the Lord's Prayer, you will learn to understand the words only when you recognise that the ship of this prayer guides you between the Tempter and Evil; guides you between too much learning, and too much working. To hold the balance, to keep the middle path, is what we have to try to achieve time and time again.

In addition, dear friends, I have tried to describe to you this ego-monogram which was impressed into our forehead when, in 3101 BC, the period of Kali Yuga began, and when the powers of the brain started to reject the inscriptions which man still made upon it by his work, and I described how these powers of rejection created a kind of concave mirror. I spoke of a phantom, dear friends, but a phantom does not mean something that has no existence. A phantom is not material but it is present; a concave mirror which focuses experiences, bringing everything towards us in such a way that we relate it egoistically to ourselves. Thus we go through life with this phantom, or figurehead as I described it yesterday. Here in the region of the forehead we experience the distorted, egoistic image of ourselves, and we have lived with this image for the last five thousand years. This image was necessary and important, for it has made it possible for us to become a self: I don't say 'an ego', but a 'self' here on earth. And now imagine the following, dear friends: learning streamed from above and working arose from below, not only into the rhythmic system, but they gradually mirrored themselves in the forehead and then from there, (from our self-monogram, from this image which we have of our existence), learning was directed and work was also directed. Now this will have to move gradually downwards from the forehead so that learning and working can begin to live in the rhythmic system. But this is not possible as long as the rhythmic system is dominated by our own distorted ego-image. As long as this is the case we are not yet able to be proclaimers, seeds, of the Threefold Commonwealth. Yet we ourselves must become members of the Threefold Commonwealth, and this we will only be able to do if *within us* we carry the free spiritual life—learning; the economic sphere—working; and the sphere of rights—not here in the head, but in the heart. Now you can understand how it was possible, throughout the last sixty, eighty, or hundred years, and still is today, to continually distort the sphere of rights, whether by imperialism, by dictatorship, or by all the terrible social aberrations which we have experienced and continue to experience. In a dictatorship we see how a group of people, or a single person, be he Mussolini, Lenin or Hitler, creates such an ego-monogram within the dictatorship government, which then carries everything in us up to this sphere of the distorted ego-image instead of uniting it with the rhythmic organisation and thereby letting flow the sphere of the spiritual life, the sphere of rights and the sphere of work. To understand this, dear friends, means to allow this ego-monogram (which is dissolving anyway) to be replaced gradually by the organ which I described to you yesterday—the organ which over the last five hundred years has been created, and which should now begin to make it possible for spiritual knowledge to be understood by human beings. This is one aspect.

Another is the following. It is one of the most tragic experiences of our time that we see within us, as well as around us, how the will and the ability to work die away. People no longer know why they ought to work, or indeed how to work. . . Increasingly workmen are unable to handle their tools, because they are simply not willing; they don't know for what or whom they work.

Dear friends, I would strongly advise to you read a short essay which Rudolf Steiner wrote during the time he sponsored the Threefold Commonwealth. It is called *Ability to Work, The Will to Work and The Threefold Social Organism.*[32] There he makes it quite clear that it is not realistic to expect that profit or gain will instil in people any kind of will to work. Since then we have experienced the truth of this. We have experienced that in spite of rising wages, in spite of the welfare state, in spite of ever-growing socialism in every country, where the workmen have a greater say in everything, the will to work and the ability to work have decreased. They have deteriorated against all the expectations of the prophets of socialism. If, for instance, you read not Marx, but Lassalles[33] or Bebel,[34] or all those who really stood for a proper socialist order, you will find that they imagined that the freedom which the workman will achieve, namely the freedom from want, will instil into him the will to work; the enthusiasm to work for the good of all men. The failure of this notion is one of the greatest disappointments we have experienced. And I say 'we', dear friends, because I was in the same boat: as a young man I also couldn't imagine other than that the freedom from want for all would inspire men with the enthusiasm to work. But just the opposite has happened. They have all turned into apathetic bourgeois, who have no will to lift an arm unless it is paid for three or four times over. The arm has become lame.

Dear friends, if you read Rudolf Steiner's essay mentioned above you will appreciate that you can't instil the will to work out of the sphere of economy and I translate:

> The sphere of economy will have no possibility to instil into man the will to produce.[35]

Again he continues with this fundamental statement:

> Only in the sphere of the free spiritual life can arise such love for the human social order as the artist, for instance, feels

toward the forming of his creations. If, however, one refuses to think about fostering such love within the sphere of the free spiritual life one better give up all striving for a new social order.[36]

What does this mean? Dear friends, it means that if the love for work is not instilled through the sphere of the free spiritual life, the work itself will no longer be done. You understand how serious this is, or at least I *hope* you understand. What has happened is the following. The wage incentive has been introduced for work done, and the wage has made possible the eradication of the other side of human existence, namely the love for work.

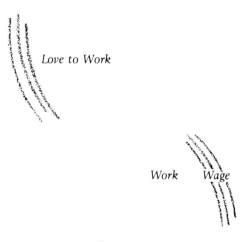

Love to Work

Work   *Wage*

Illustration 31

All that is left is the wage-earner and the wage-payer, and therefore the fundamental social law which we all know cannot come into play any more:

> There is then, a fundamental social law which anthroposophy teaches us and which is as follows: In a community of human beings working together, the well-being of the community will be the greater, the less the individual claims for himself the proceeds of the work he has himself done;

i.e., the more of these proceeds he makes over to his fellow-workers, and the more his own requirements are satisfied, not out of his own work done, but out of work done by the others.[37]

Dear friends, this should not only be studied, it should be made a continuous exercise, in order to overcome the complete idiocy of today's economic structure which is ingrained in every one of us. Whenever we think of the economic order, we think in terms of income and expenditure. I don't mean now that you should change your bookkeeping. It is quite a good exercise to write everything down, because income is based *on work*, but weaving between work and income there stands the human being.

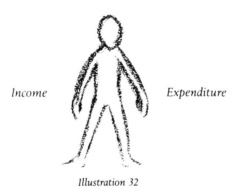

Income　　　　　　　　　　　　Expenditure

Illustration 32

Income, expenditure; income, expenditure: this is quite wrong according to the fundamental social law. (I am exercising my thoughts with you, dear friends; spiritual exercises, so to speak.) The Fundamental Social Law is thus: I work: full stop. This work then streams up and disappears, and all the other people gain from this work, live on this work. They don't live—and neither do I—on my income. Nor do I live because I have the possibility to expend something. I work, and they live. They work, and I live. And here beats the heart of society and the heart of man. Certainly as long as money still represents wages and profit, books must be kept according to income and expenditure. There is no way out.

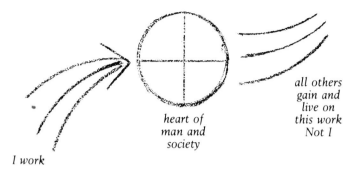

*heart of
man and
society*

*all others
gain and
live on
this work
Not I*

I work

Illustration 33

Another very important question for our villages is the following: What place does religion have in our life? I cannot help but say religion is important. It is necessary that our life is permeated by religion, permeated by the grace of the Sacraments. But if we look again at the archetypal image which we have now gained, permit me to say the following. Religion permeates the sphere of rights, builds the basis for the sphere of work, as well as for the sphere of the free spiritual life.

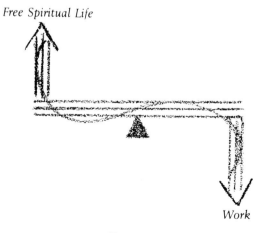

Free Spiritual Life

Work

Illustration 34

The fulcrum, would be about here. But the free spiritual life is different from religion, and the sphere of work is also different. The sphere of the free spiritual life is the sphere of the Holy Spirit, and no religious exercise, neither Bible Evening nor Sunday service, will help to unfold this organ which five hundred years ago was laid as a seed into the forebrain of man, if we want to create a new will to work and a new ability to work. During the first ten years our young friends can work out of enthusiasm, out of the way we live together. We must now begin (and you have already begun) to create a sphere of the free spiritual life which will make it possible for our young people to bring the ability, the skill, the enthusiasm for work to the workshops, to the farms and wherever they have to exercise their working capacity. But looking ahead we have to establish a true sphere of the spiritual life, *which is not the sphere of religion.* The sphere of the free spiritual life is something special. To me it appears, and I am very careful in saying this, that we must make everyone who lives with us understand the fundamentals of Goetheanism. Without this the awakening powers of spiritual thinking cannot be exercised. We must learn to understand in an immediate image how the seed unfolds into leaf, the leaf into flower, the flower into fruit; how the living, formative forces are working through a plant; how the leaf is the archetypal form in every plant, whether it is flower or stem, or whether it is node, root or fruit: we must begin to exercise this. And then for instance, a poem such as *The Metamorphosis of Plants* by Goethe should be studied, or some of Goethe's writings—which are translated, perfectly translated by an English botanist. These should be studied—but not hammered in, that's not necessary. Our young people *are* able to understand the principles of metamorphosis, and to see how the formative forces work and transform. To exercise these fundamental ideas, to work on them, though not in an intellectual way is, I think, one of the most important steps we should make in order to create in every one of the villagers a sphere of the free spiritual life. To take up, for instance, George Adams' work on Point and Sphere, and to exercise this by drawing and painting, or to take a book like *The Plant Between Sun and Earth*[38] and to look at these pictures with our young people and let them be experienced, will enable you to see what it will bring about. If this is done, dear friends, then we take the next step, the step to the great metamorphosis of all existence; the metamorphosis of incarnation and reincarnation. We not only speak about it, but we *carry it within ourselves* and make it a kind of need and a matter of course, a foregone conclusion; something which cannot be argued about, because it *is* so, it *is* the reality. Only when you begin to do this will you be able to fill the sphere of the spiritual life, which you have built on Goetheanism, with its real content. Read the very important lecture which Rudolf Steiner gave on the 21st February 1912, a lecture which we cannot often enough take to heart. Read the whole lecture in order to *understand* what he means. He says there, for instance:

> The complexity of external life will steadily increase and however many activities are taken over from man in the future by machines, there can be very few lives of happiness in this present incarnation unless conditions quite different from those now prevailing are brought about. And these different conditions must be the result of *the human soul being convinced of the truth of reincarnation and karma.*[39]

Rudolf Steiner said this in 1912, before the First World War. He continues:

> And it is incumbent upon those who call themselves anthroposophists today to play their part in ensuring that the truths of reincarnation and karma shall flow even into the minds of the young. This of course does not mean that anthroposophists who have children should inculcate this into them as dogma. *Insight* is what is needed.[40]

Dear friends, he compares the idea of karma and reincarnation in this lecture with the Copernican idea and he says:

> Who can possibly doubt that Copernicanism has taken firm root, even in the minds of children?—I am not speaking now of its truths and its errors. If culture is not to fall into decline, the truths of reincarnation and karma must take equally firm root—but the time that humanity has at its disposal for this is not as long as it was in the case of Copernicanism.[41]

Now again, with our handicapped friends, with our handicapped children, we can—if we ourselves are enthused with this idea in the way Rudolf Steiner means—simply take it into daily life, within the sphere of the free spiritual life, and there it should be exercised. We have a great number of examples which Rudolf Steiner has given: why should we not use them? There is no reason to keep them under the counter, so to speak, to be taken out only for those who show their Membership Card of the Anthroposophical Society. It is ridiculous to have such an attitude. You see, for instance, Rudolf Steiner says in these lectures on karma:

> What can you do? You can only tell tales. Because intellectually you can't explain it: it's quite impossible. You can't say because this was, that has come about.[42]

But you can tell the story of a man like Pestalozzi.[43] What more beautiful story could you tell? Relate the life of Pestalozzi, the great teacher, the great benefactor of children and men who lived at the end of the eighteenth and the beginning of the nineteenth century. This wonderfully mild personality, with the great heart, whose efforts and attempts were always thwarted; yet what an impact he made on the thousands who were around him! And then to know that in the first century before Christ, somewhere in the south of Europe (probably in one of the Greek colonies) that he was an overseer of a number of slaves, and that even then he had a very good heart. He was a very educated man for his time, and he wanted to extend the good to the men and women who were given into his care, because many of them were Greek, were educated people. But above him was his master, and this master was a rough man, who through the overseer did many misdeeds towards this colony of slaves. Thus this individuality stood between the group of people whom he loved and the master who exercised draconian measures through him. And beside him stood his wife. Then came another incarnation in the ninth century in which he was a woman, and as a woman was destined to be the wife of the one who had previously been the master. It wasn't a happy relationship, because the master now lived in a small community of people, in a little town, and the people now exacted on him what he had done to them in the previous incarnation. Again this personality, now as the wife, had to suffer; had to suffer with her husband, the former master, for what had been done in the previous life. When they reincarnated, the wife, who previously had been with the overseer, now became Pestalozzi, and the whole colony of slaves was around him; they were the children whom he helped, the young people whom he educated. What more wonderful story could one tell? This would fill the free spiritual life, because these are the new fairy tales which we can tell when we do so in devotion of heart and with the earnestness which such a story demands.

Or what more wonderful story could one tell than that of the Viennese dramatist, writer and actor, Ferdinand Raimund,[43] who lived a very short life for he was not more than forty-two or forty-three years old when he shot himself. He shot himself yet he didn't die immediately but succumbed a few days later to the severe wound which he had inflicted on himself. He was a genius. Rudolf Steiner once called him the only one on the continent of Europe whom we can compare with the genius of Shakespeare in the plays he wrote. Nothing could be more wonderful than to enact one of his plays in one or other of our villages, and then to know his background. Once upon a time this individuality lived in the Near East, (probably in India or Afghanistan) in a community of people in which the worship of animals was at its height, and where every animal was cared for and loved. This individuality lived among them, yet he was possessed by the drive to torture animals, even to kill them. Thereby he was driven increasingly into complete social isolation, and because he was in reality one of those who worshipped animals, more and more this inner urge made him utterly lonely. He was reborn, as Raimund, with the urge to keep animals around him because he was filled with fear of loneliness, with anxiety, and so he always had a dog, a cat, anything that could be kept in Vienna. He even went so far as to let these animals eat out of the same plate from which he was eating, not knowing why. As soon as this happened, he was seized by tremendous fear that he would contract the illness of the animal. The last straw was when the dog with whom he had shared food suddenly appeared to have rabies: he saw no way out but to shoot himself.

Dear friends, these are examples which we have to take up. We can turn to all this, if we do not ask out of curiosity, 'Who was this or that man?' but if we stand with awe before such images and hand them over, as during the Middle Ages the Rosicrucians went about and gave out fairy tale after fairy tale, proverb after proverb, thereby educating the morality of people through images and pictures. We certainly can do it. I have the impression that it is the way to build up the sphere of the free spiritual life. Many more things can be done—these are just examples—if you do them in the form of a tale not in the form of an intellectual exercise where you weigh up why this has been, or why that has happened. You will more and more create in our young friends, and through them in thousands of people, the image of the Representative of Man, which is the image of the new social order, the image of the Threefold Commonwealth, because he bears the name, 'Michael, the countenance of Christ'. If we learn to understand this, and out of understanding to practice it, and out of practicing it to conduct our life and the life of those around us, then the pilot experiment, the little seed of the Threefold Commonwealth, might gradually grow and spread healing into the illness of our existence and time. Let this be a kind of rounding-off to what I have tried to tell you during the last two days. Thank you.

Appendix A

Rudolf Steiner. Quotation taken from the lecture given on 18th October, 1918. In: *From Symptom to Reality in Modern History*. Rudolf Steiner Press, London 1976. 9 lectures, 18th October–3th November, 1918, Dornach. G.A. 185.

'Today, however, there is one field of investigation which operates with very inadequate means and is as yet in its very early stages, but which is calculated to give valuable information about human nature, namely the study of pathological conditions in man. When we study the case history of a man who is not quite normal we feel that we can be at one with him; that with sympathetic understanding we can break through the barrier that separates us from him and so draw nearer to him. By experimentation we are detached from reality; by the study of what are called today pathological conditions—malformations as Goethe so aptly called them—we are brought back to reality. We must not be repelled by them, but must develop an understanding for them. We must say to ourselves: the tragic element in life—without ever wishing it for anybody—can sometimes be most instructive; it can throw a flood of light upon the deepest mysteries of life. We shall only understand the significance of the brain for the life of the soul through a more intensive study of the mentally disturbed. And this is the training ground for a sympathetic understanding of others. Life uses the crude instrument of sickness in order to awaken our interest in others. It is this concern for our neighbour which can promote the social progress of mankind in the immediate future, whereas the reverse of positiveness, a superficial attitude of sympathy or antipathy towards others, makes for social regression. These things are all related to the mystery of the epoch of the consciousness soul.'

Appendix B

Rudolf Steiner. Quotation taken from a lecture entitled: *How can the psychological distress of today be overcome?* In: *Spiritual Research: Methods and Results.* Steinerbooks, Blauvelt, New York, 1981. G.A. 168.

'When the science of spirit grows more and more away from abstraction into concrete life there will appear, among the circles which occupy themselves with this science of spirit, a special kind of human understanding, a way of awakening human interest. There will then be people who have certain capacities for teaching their fellow men about the different human temperaments, about the different human dispositions; how a man with this or that temperament should be treated, and how another man with a disposition of that kind, or with that temperament, must be treated in another way. Men who have a special gift for this will teach other men, who are to learn from them, such things as this: Look carefully, there exist this and that type of human being, and one must treat one man in one way, and the other in another. A practical psychology, a practical study of the soul and of life, will be cultivated and a truly social understanding of human evolution will result.'

Appendix C

Sheldon's Scale for Temperament

I: Viscerotonia.	II: Somatotonia.	III: Cerebrotonia.
1. Relaxation in Posture and Movement	Assertiveness of Posture and Movement	Restraint in Posture and Movement, Tightness
2. Love of Physical Comfort	Love of Physical Adventure	Physiological Over-response
3. Slow Reaction	The Energetic Characteristics	Overly Fast Reactions
4. Love of Eating	Need and Enjoyment of Exercise	Love of Privacy
5. Socialization of Eating	Love of Dominating, Lust for Power	Mental Over-intensity, Hyperattentionality, Apprehensiveness
6. Pleasure in Digestion	Love of Risk and Chance	Secretiveness of Feeling, Emotional Restraint
7. Love of Polite Ceremony	Bold Directness of Manner	Self-Conscious Motility of the Eyes and Face
8. Sociophilia	Physical Courage for Combat	Sociophobia
9. Indiscriminate Amiability	Competitive Aggressiveness	Inhibited Social Address
10. Greed for Affection and Approval	Psychological Callousness	Resistance to Habit, and Poor Routinizing

IN NEED OF SPECIAL UNDERSTANDING

11.	Orientation to People	Claustrophobia	Agoraphobia
12.	Evenness of Emotional Flow	Ruthlessness, Freedom from Sqeamishness	Unpredictability of Attitude
13.	Tolerance	The Unrestrained Voice	Vocal Restraint and General Restraint of Noise
14.	Complacency	Spartan Indifference to Pain	Hypersensitivity to Pain
15.	Deep Sleep	General Noisiness	Poor Sleep Habits, Chronic Fatigue
16.	The Untempered Characteristic	Overmaturity of Appearance	Youthful Intentness of Manner and Appearance
17.	Smooth, Easy Communication of Feeling, Extraversion of Visceratonia	Horizontal Mental Cleavage, Extraversion of Somototonia	Vertical Mental Cleavage, Introversion
18.	Relaxation and Sociophilia under Alcohol	Assertiveness and Aggression under Alcohol	Resistance to Alcohol, and to other Depressant Drugs
19.	Need of People when Troubled	Need of Action when Troubled	Need of Solitude when Troubled
20.	Orientation toward Childhood and Family Relationships	Orientation toward Goals and Activities of Youth	Orientation toward the Later Periods of Life

References

1: Rudolf Steiner. *Anthroposophie. Ein Fragment.* 1910. G.A. 45

2: Gustav Schwab. *Der Reiter uberm Bodensee*—a well known German poem.

3: Rudolf Steiner. *Weihnachts Kurs für Lehrer.* 16 lectures, 23rd December 1921–7th January 1922, Dornach. G.A. 303. *Lectures to Teachers,* trans. D. Harwood, Anthroposophical Publishing Co. London, 1948. (Reference is to 13th lecture, given on 4th January, 1922.)

4: Marcel Proust, 1871–1922. *A la Recherche du Temps Perdu* published between 1913 and 1927 in seven subtitled volumes. *Rememberance of Things Past.* 3 Vols., trans. C.K.S. Moncrieff and T. Kilmartin, Chatto, London 1981, and Penguin 1983. The *Encyclopaedia Britannica* states . . .his people are never given as ´characters` in the fashion of Balzac, they are always in the process of development, change and continual creation.

5: Selections have since been translated by Owen Barfield under the title *The Case for Anthroposophy,* Rudolf Steiner Press, London, 1970. The chapter in question is entitled 'Principles of Psychosomatic Physiology'.

6: Della Porta, Giovanni Battista, 1538–1615. Born Naples of ancient nobility, natural philosopher, travelled extensively in Italy, Spain, France. Published *Magia natura sive de miraculis rerum naturalium* 1589, in twenty volumes.

7: Lavater, Johann Kaspar, 1741–1801, Swiss protestant theologian, poet, mystic, physiognomist, friend of Goethe who contributed a chapter to the work for which Lavater is best known, *Physiognomical Fragments to advance the knowledge of Man and Love among Humanity* 1775–1778.

197

8: Kretschmer, Ernst, 1888–1964. Professor of Neurology and Psychiatry at Marburg University. Medical Director of the Marburg University Psychiatric Hospital. A prolific writer. Kretschmer distinguishes three constitutional types: Asthenic, Athletic and Pyknik, the 'Athletic' being most closely related to Sheldon's Mesomorph (Somatotonic).

9: Sheldon, Win. H., Ph.D., M.D. born 1899. *The Varieties of Temperament. A Psychology of Constitutional Differences*. Harvard University. Harper Brothers, New York and London, 1942. This book is best read in conjunction with Sheldon's *Atlas of Men. A Guide to Somatotyping the Adult Male at all ages*. Department of Medicine, College of Physicians & Surgeons, Universities of Columbia and Oregon. Gramercy Publishing Co., New York.

10: Rudolf Steiner. *Menschenschicksale und Völkerschicksale*. 12 lectures, between 1st September 1914 and 6th July 1915, Berlin. G.A. 157. Available in English as typescript only entitled *Thoughts for the Times*. Bibliographical Reference List of the Works of Rudolf Steiner Translated in English, compiled by Craig Giddens.

11: Rudolf Steiner. *Welt, Erde und Mensch*. 11 lectures, 4th–16th August 1908, Stuttgart. G.A. 105. *Universe, Earth and Man*. Rudolf Steiner Publishing Co., London, 1955. (Lectures referred to are numbers 1 & 2 of 4th & 5th August).

12: Rudolf Steiner. *Grundlinien einer okkulten Psychologie*. 11 lectures, 23rd September–16th October 1921, Dornach. Now found under the title *Anthroposophie als Kosmosophie: Erste Tiel* G.A. 207. *Cosmosophy. Vol. I* Anthroposophic Press, New York, 1985. (Lectures referred to are 30th September and 2nd October 1921).

13: Rudolf Steiner. *Man and Woman in the Light of Spiritual Science*. Munich, 18th March 1908. G.A. 56. *Anthroposophical Review*, Vol.2, No. I, Winter 1980.

14: Rudolf Steiner. *Weihnachts Kurs für Lehrer*. 16 lectures, 23rd December 1921–7th January 1922, Dornach. G.A. 303. *Lectures to Teachers*, trans. D. Harwood, Anthroposophical Publishing Co. London, 1948. (Reference is to 13th lecture, given on 4th January, 1922.)

REFERENCES

15: Rudolf Steiner. *Anthroposophie und das menschliche Gemüt.* 4 lectures, 27th September–1st October 1923, Vienna. G.A. 223. *Michaelmas and the Soul-Forces of Man.* Anthroposophic Press, New York, 1982.

16: Rudolf Steiner. *Anthroposophische Lebensgaben.* 14th May 1918, Berlin. G.A. 181.

17: *ibid.*

18: *ibid.*

19: *ibid.*

20: *ibid.*

21: Rudolf Steiner. *Das Karma des Berufes des Menschen in Anknüpfung an Goethes Leben.* 10 lectures, 4th–27th November 1916, Dornach. G.A. 172. *The Karma of Vocation.* Anthroposophic Press, New York, 1984.

22: Rudolf Steiner. *The Philosophy of Freedom.* Rudolf Steiner Press, London, 1964. G.A. 4. Also published under the original title *The Philosophy of Spiritual Activity.* Anthroposophic Press, New York, 1984.

23: Rudolf Steiner. *Knowledge of the Higher Worlds–How is it Achieved?* Rudolf Steiner Press, London, 1969. G.A. 10. Available also as *Knowledge of the Higher Worlds and Its Attainment.* Anthroposophic Press, New York.

24: Rudolf Steiner. *Innere Entwicklungsimpulse der Menschheit. Goethe und die Krisis des neunzehnten Jahrhunderts.* 16 lectures, 16th September–30th October 1916, Dornach. G.A. 171.

25: Rudolf Steiner. *Das Karma des Berufes des Menschen in Anknüpfung an Goethes Leben.* 10 lectures, 4th–27th November 1916, Dornach. G.A. 172. *The Karma of Vocation.* Anthroposophic Press, New York, 1984. (see pp. 102–103).

26: *ibid.*, pp. 103–104.

27: *ibid.*, pp. 104–105.

28: *ibid.,* pp. 105–106.

For further reading in connection with the foregoing lectures see also:

Rudolf Steiner. *Kosmische und menschliche Geschichte, Band 1–7: Das Karma des Berufes des Menschen in Anknüpfung an Goethes Leben.* Compilation of lectures given in Dornach between 29th July 1916 and 21st March 1921. G.A. 170–174b.

29: Rudolf Steiner. *Die okkulten Grundlagen der Bhagavad Gita.* 9 Lectures, 28th May–5th June 1913, Helsingfors. G.A. 146. *The Occult Significance of the Bhagavad Gita.* Anthroposophic Press, New York, 1984.

30: *ibid.,* pp. 68–69.

31: *ibid.,* p. 71.

32: Rudolf Steiner. *Arbeitsfähigkeit, Arbeitswille und dreigliediger sozialer Organismus.* In: *Aufsätze über die Dreigliederung des Sozialen Organismus und zur Zeitlage, 1915–1921.* G.A. 24.

33: Lassalles, Ferdinand (1825–1864).
A fascinating, brilliant career, deeply devoted to democratic freedoms, wrote several important books on subjects of Philosophy, Law, Politics. His historic deed is the founding of the Social Democratic Labour Association. His youthful enthusiasm overcame tremendous obstacles but also carried him to his death in a duel over the love of a woman.

34: Bebel, August (1840–1913).
A strong and convincing personality, he was for many years the most popular leader of the Labour Movement. Inspired by Lassalles he joined in building up the Social Democratic Labour Association. He was an opponent of Bismarck's policies and was imprisoned several times. Several books and brilliant speeches bear witness to his deep devotion to the socialist cause nationally and internationally.

35: Rudolf Steiner. *Arbeitsfähigkeit, Arbeitswille und dreigliediger sozialer Organismus.* In: *Aufsätze über die Dreigliederung des Sozialen Organismus und zur Zeitlage, 1915–1921.* G.A. 24.

36: *ibid.*

37: Rudolf Steiner. *Geisteswissenschaft und Soziale Frage.* Essay published in *Lucifer-Gnosis,* Berlin, 1905. Translated as *Anthroposophy and The Social Question.* Anthroposophic Press, New York, 1958. G.A. 34.

38: Adams, George and Whicher, Olive. *The Plant between Sun and Earth.* Goethean Science Foundation, Clent, 1952.

39: Rudolf Steiner. *Reincarnation and Karma: their significance in Modern Culture.* Five lectures, January–March 1912, Berlin and Stuttgart. Steiner Book Centre, N. Vancouver, 1977. G.A. 135.

40: *ibid.*

41: *ibid.*

42: *ibid.*

Lecture IV, from which the quotes are taken, closes with these words:
The anthroposophist must feel and be conscious of the fact that in this way he is helping to bring about the birth of a new culture. This feeling of the enormous significance in life of the ideas of reincarnation and karma can be a bond of union among a group of human beings today, no matter what their external circumstances may be. And those who are eventually held together by such a feeling can find their way to one another only through Anthroposophy.

43: Pestalozzi, Johann Heinrich (1746–1827).
Swiss educator and reformer. As a youth associated with Lavater, politically active in the 'Party of Reform'. Deeply interested in education, in which he found his life's task. His book *Leonard and Gertrude* (1781) established his name internationally as an educational reformer. There exist a considerable number of books on his work and educational theories.
See Rudolf Steiner: *Karmic Relationships: Vol II.* 16 lectures, 6th April–29th June 1924, Dornach. G.A. 236. (Reference is to lecture of 23rd April, 1924.)

44: Raimund, Ferdinand (1790–1836).
Austrian Dramatist. See Rudolf Steiner: *Kursus für Pastoralmedizin.* 11 lectures, 8th–18th September 1924, Dornach. G.A. 318. (Reference is to lecture of 13th September, 1924.)

Other titles by Karl König

Rudolf Steiner's Calendar of the Soul — A Commentary
Translated by E.H. Goddard and A.C. Harwood.
Rudolf Steiner Press, London 1977.
ISBN 0 85440 314 0

The Human Soul
Floris Books, Edinburgh 1986.
ISBN 0 86315 042 X

Brothers and Sisters — the order of birth in the family
Floris Books, Edinburgh 1984.
ISBN 0 903540 38 X

The First Three Years of the Child
Translated by Carlo Pietzner
Floris Books, Edinburgh 1984.
ISBN 0 86315 011 X

Illnesses of Our Time
Kolisko Archive Publications, Bournemouth 1979.
ISBN 0 906492 36 X

The Handicapped Child — letters to parents
Camphill Press, Whitby 1982.
ISBN 0 904145 32 8

A Christmas Story
Camphill Press, Whitby 1984.
ISBN 0 904145 24 7

Penguins, Seals, Dolphins, Salmon and Eels
Floris Books, Edinburgh 1984.
ISBN 0 86315 014 4

Swans and Storks, Sparrows and Doves
Floris Books, Edinburgh 1986.
ISBN 0 86315 046 2

Earth and Man
Edited by Hartmut von Jeetze
Bio-Dynamic Literature, Rhode Island 1982
ISBN 0 938250 1813

Plays for Christmas
Translated by Anke Weihs
Camphill Press, Whitby 1980.
ISBN 0 904145 20 4

An Easter Play — Prologue and Part I
Translated by Anke Weihs
Camphill Press, Whitby 1981.
ISBN 0 904145 21 2

An Easter Play — Parts II and III
Translated by Anke Weihs
Camphill Press, Whitby 1981.
ISBN 0 904145 22 0

Plays for Ascentiontide
Translated by Anke Weihs
Camphill Press, Whitby 1981.
ISBN 0 904145 23 9

Festival Plays
Translated by Anke Weihs
Camphill Press, Whitby 1984.
ISBN 0 904145 25 5

The Camphill Movement
Camphill Press, Whitby 1981.
ISBN 0 904145 30 1